THE WARFARE
WITH
SATAN

THE WARFARE

WITH

SATAN

AND THE WAY OF VICTORY

By

Jessie Penn-Lewis

CHRISTIAN • LITERATURE • CRUSADE
Fort Washington, Pennsylvania 19034

CHRISTIAN LITERATURE CRUSADE

U.S.A.
P.O. Box 1449, Fort Washington, PA 19034

BRITAIN
51 The Dean, Alresford, Hants SO24 9BJ

AUSTRALIA
P.O. Box 91, Pennant Hills N.S.W. 2120

NEW ZEALAND
126 Broadway, Palmerston North

This American edition revised and reset
1993.

Cover picture —SuperStock

ISBN   0-87508-731-0

PRINTED IN THE UNITED STATES OF AMERICA

CONTENTS

PREFACE

THIS book is based on a series of addresses given by Mrs. Penn-Lewis in 1897, at a day of waiting on God at the C.I.M. Hall, London. Since then a number of editions have been printed, and it has proved of value to many Christian workers.

In her original preface, Mrs. Penn-Lewis wrote: "So little has been written on this subject from an experiential standpoint that I trust the following brief treatise dealing with a vast and to a certain extent little-known subject may be of practical service at this present time to all who are meeting the forces of darkness with what is to them new power."

In sending out this edition, our prayer is that this book may be used to bring light, hope and victory to many in all sections of the Christian Church.

J.C. Metcalfe

Parkstone,
Dorset,
May 1973

CHAPTER ONE

The Risen Lord in the midst of His people and His call to victory.

THE Apostle John had been banished to Patmos "for the word of God and the testimony to Jesus." It seemed that his work for the Master was ended! But in the plan of the Omnipotent Lord it turned out to be greater and wider service than he had ever dreamed of, and more far-reaching in its effects than any previous part of his life. On the lonely isle, cut off from all intercourse with other children of God, the Lord appeared to him as the Glorified One enthroned on the right hand of the Majesty on high, choosing him to be the channel for transmitting to His people a direct revelation of His heart and will concerning them. He gave him a wondrous unveiling of the history and destiny of the Church of the redeemed, the concluding scenes of which would wind up the dealings of God with the planet and usher in the glorious reign of the Son of God upon the earth.

It is written that the Apocalypse is the Revelation of Jesus Christ, which God gave unto Him, to show

unto His servants the things which must shortly
come to pass (1:1, mar.). But He must find a human
channel to convey it to His people. So it was for this
purpose that the King of kings permitted the devil to
arouse the persecution which transferred His chosen
vessel to the lonely isle; there, away from the claims of
active service, John would be free to receive the
message from on high. Unfavorable circumstances
can only come to the redeemed of the Lord so far as
they are necessary for the fulfillment of His plans.

The apostle is "in the Spirit on the Lord's day,"
and suddenly hears a great voice saying, "What
thou seest, write in a book, and send it to the seven
churches." He turns to see who it is that speaks to
him, and there breaks upon his spiritual vision a
wondrous revelation of Him whom he had known
on earth as the Man Christ Jesus, the very One he
had seen hanging upon a cross of shame, despised
and rejected of men, the One he had talked with
after His resurrection, the very same Jesus he had
seen pass into the clouds of heaven.

John sees Him "in the midst of the lampstands,"
which are explained later on to be the seven
churches (1:20, mar.). He is seen to be walking in
the midst—walking as He walked in the temple at
Jerusalem, first a silent onlooker, and then a
cleanser of all that defiled His Father's house. It
was written of Him, "Zeal for Thy house shall eat
Me up" (John 2:17).

The Glorified Lord was clothed in garments de-
noting His High Priesthood within the veil. He
went as a forerunner for us, having become a High
Priest forever after the order of Melchizedek, and
there He ever lives to make intercession for all who

draw near to God through Him. The golden girdle
He wears denotes the investiture of highest rank
and power. His head and hair are white as white
wool, signifying purity rather than age. It is re-
markable that the same characteristic of hair like
pure wool was seen by Daniel when he had the
vision of the One who sat upon a throne of fiery
flames, when the judgment was set and the books
were opened (Dan. 7:9–10). "Glorify Thou Me with
Thine own self with the glory which I had with
Thee before the world was," prayed the God-man
on the eve of His passion. The Father and the Son
are One. The Ancient of Days and the Christ who
appeared to John, with head and hair as white as
wool, are One—blessed for evermore.

The apostle says that "His eyes were as a flame
of fire," all-searching and consuming, and "His feet
like unto burnished brass, as if it had been refined
in a *furnace*." Fire is His very essence of being: fire
of love toward perishing sinners; fire of wrath upon
sin; fire which consumes, and melts and burns all
that is not of its own nature so as to transform all it
touches into its own element. The Man on the
throne had "the appearance of fire" (Ezek. 1:27),
when Ezekiel saw Him, and the Man who appeared
to Daniel had eyes as "lamps of fire" (Dan. 10:6).
Yes, our God is a consuming fire.

"His voice as the voice of many waters," is always
sweet to His Bride, but terrible to those who do not
know Him. "Out of His mouth proceeded a sharp
two-edged sword," for His mouth gives forth words
"living, and active, and sharper than any two-
edged sword," and "piercing even to the dividing
of soul and spirit, of both joints and marrow, and

quick to discern the thoughts and intents of the heart" (Heb. 4:12). Yes, His word acts as a sacrificial knife in all who yield to Him, and are laid upon the altar of His cross in fellowship with Him—there to be consumed by the heavenly fire—a whole burnt-offering to God.

But what words could describe His face? John says, "His countenance was as the sun shineth in his strength." Who can gaze into the face of the sun which was created by Him, and who can look with undimmed vision into His face as it is now in glory? He bears a face which was once more marred than any man's—so marred that when it is revealed to seeking souls as that of "God manifest in the flesh," He startles nations (Isa. 52:14–15, mar.).

The apostle saw the Son of Man, His clothing, His girdle, His hair, His eyes, His feet, and heard the voice that spoke to him like a trumpet, or the sound of many waters; but when his eyes were raised, and he looked full in His face and saw Him, then he fell at His feet as one dead.

If the apostle, who knew Him on earth so well that he leaned upon His bosom in intimate fellowship and love, thus fell before Him at the sight of His heavenly glory, what shall it be for those who reject Him now? Even kings of the earth and princes shall cry, "Hide us from the face of Him that sitteth on the throne, and from the wrath of the Lamb."

But to the apostle it was the very same Jesus that he had known on earth. He had not changed. The glory of that light which was always in Him, as shown on the Mount when He was transfigured before them, face shining as the sun, now shone out unveiled by the body of His humanity. He is still

Man—the Son of Man—in the glory, as He quickly showed when He saw His beloved apostle lying prostrate at His feet.

How often the touch of His hand on earth had healed and blessed. How sweetly His voice had said again and again, "Fear not—it is I, be not afraid"; and once more the familiar words "Fear not" break on the ear of the prostrate man. He lies "as one dead," unable to help himself. Daniel also so lay when, at the sight of the Lord of glory with eyes as lamps of fire, his earth-born comeliness was turned into corruption; he fell into a deep sleep, his face toward the ground, until a hand touched him and strengthened him to hear the divine words. The same hand, but now a hand which John had seen pierced and nailed to the cross, is laid upon the apostle on Patmos, while the familiar voice speaks the old calming words, "Fear not." "Fear not; I am the First and the Last." The beginning of all things, and the end of all the purposes of God. Changeless from all eternity. Manifest in the flesh. Received up into glory. I am

THE LIVING ONE.

"I became dead, and behold, I am alive unto the ages of the ages" (1:18, mar.). "Fear not, John, remember Calvary. You saw Me there. You beheld My passion there. You gazed upon the marred face, and the smitten form. You saw the hour and power of darkness working through the creatures of My hands. You saw Me in My resurrection body, and conversed with Me after My rising from the dead. But now, behold Me as I am in the glory which I had with the Father before the world was; and know that I who became dead for your sake am now alive forevermore, and have the keys to death and the grave. Through death I have brought to nought him who had the power of death. O death, where is your victory? O death, where is your sting?"

Why did the Lord of glory thus appear to John? He who had sent the Holy Spirit to lead His redeemed ones into all the truth now sends to them the call from heaven to overcome!

No message is sent to the unbelieving world, for God had already spoken by His Son and given the full manifestation of His love to sinners in His death on Calvary. But an after-message comes from the Glorified Lord in heaven to His own people. He had watched them in all their various circumstances and noted their trials and temptations. He had walked in their midst and seen the Holy Spirit grieved and oft-times quenched—the still, small voice unheeded, the warning touch unnoticed, the restraining providence unknown. He had observed the active service and the decline of deep personal love to Him. He had noted with tenderness the tribulation and poverty of some and the dwelling even "where Satan's throne is" of others. He who had conquered Satan at Calvary had watched the "deep things of Satan" being taught to His servants—some with a reputation of being alive, yet actually dead before Him, and others lukewarm and self-satisfied. Yes, He had watched it all, and once more spoke from heaven to awaken His people, to bid them overcome. His chosen vessel is drawn aside to wait before Him. The cloud which received Him out of sight once more opens, the veil is drawn aside, and the Lord of glory appears.

"What you see, write in a book, and send it to

the seven churches" is the command. Tell them the "things which you *saw*"—I am walking in their midst with eyes of fire; tell them "the things which *are*"—I am the Risen Lord, High Priest of My people, and I know their ways; and *"the things which shall come to pass hereafter"*—when they overcome they shall reign with Me and "sit down with Me in My Throne, as I also overcame and sat down with My Father on His Throne" (Rev. 3:21).

May the Lord's sevenfold command reach every reader: "He who has an ear—the ear of the new creation formed within—let him hear what the Spirit says to the churches."

CHAPTER TWO

*The adversary: his origin; his names;
his kingdom; his organized government; and
his religion.*

BEFORE we can understand the meaning of the urgent call to overcome, sent to His people by the Risen Lord through His Apostle John, it is necessary that we should see something of the prince of darkness and his kingdom. Our first question must be: who is the prince of darkness and where did he come from? The Scriptures give but veiled glimpses of his origin and home. The purpose of Scripture is more expressly to reveal God and His Christ as the Redeemer of men, the history of the redeemed from the fall of Adam in Eden, the way of salvation through the cross, and the eternal destiny of God's children—when the Christ shall have "abolished all rule and all authority and power" (1 Cor. 15:24) contrary to the reign of God, and God Himself shall be All in All.

It is generally understood that the prophet Isaiah referred primarily to the adversary of God and man when he said "How art thou fallen from heaven, O day star, son of the morning! . . . thou saidst in thine heart . . . I will exalt my throne above the stars of God . . . I will be like the Most High. Yet thou shalt be brought down to hell, to the uttermost parts of the pit" (Isa. 14:12–15; see also 24:21 and 34:4).

We can never quite understand how it could be that among the angels there should come the thought of self. There was one into whom pride entered. He saw the wonderful glory of God in him, and began to exalt himself. He gathered others around him, and whither did this lead? It changed these angels into devils of hell. It made the fiery flames of heaven into flames of hell—the same flame, but separate from God.[1]

The Lord Jesus, speaking of the devil to the Jews, said that he *"abode* not in the truth" (John 8:44, KJV), implying that at some previous time he had been of different character. "He was a murderer from the beginning" (ibid) said the Lord, the word "beginning" being the same word used in John 1:1; the apostle repeats the expression later, saying, "The devil sinneth from the beginning" (1 John 3:8). There was a moment, then, when Satan left the "truth," and sin was found in him. There are many who think that the lament of the Lord God over the fall of a being "full of wisdom and perfect in beauty," an "anointed cherub," dwelling upon "the holy mountain of God," and walking "up and down in the midst of the stones of fire" (see Ezek. 28:11–17) refers to the fallen angel. Whether or not this is so, sufficient is said to show that back in the past ages a terrible catastrophe occurred among the angels of God, because one glorious being admitted into his heart the thought of self, and said "I"! "*I* will ascend"— "*I* will exalt my throne"—"*I* will be like the Most High." When he fell other angels fell with him, some of whom were left at large with him. However, others, who "kept not their own principality" but "left their proper habitation" (Jude 6), were cast "down to hell, and committed to pits of darkness, to be reserved unto judgment" (2 Peter 2:4).

It seems clear therefore that the prince of darkness is one who was once a beautiful archangel of the highest rank in heaven, but fell from the truth and became the very embodiment of a lie. "There is no truth in him . . . he is a liar, and the father of it" said the Lord, and the various names by which he is described in the Scriptures reveal still more of his position and character. Fallen though Satan be, the Lord Jesus, no less than three times, calls him by the title of "prince of this world" (John 12:31; 14:30; 16:11), thus plainly recognizing his authority and his official position of rule over the earth. We learn from Jude that Satan is a high personage of rank and power: "Michael the archangel, when contending with the devil he disputed about the body of Moses, *durst not* bring against him a railing judgment, but said, *The Lord* rebuke thee" (Jude 9). He is also called the "god of this age" (2 Cor. 4:4, mar.), for men obey and worship him, even unconsciously, when they do not obey and worship the Creator.

The fallen archangel is moreover described as the "prince of the power of the air" (Eph. 2:2), more literally "the prince of the aerial host," meaning wicked spiritual powers dwelling in the aerial heavens, for the "satanic confederation has its seat in the atmospheric heaven—in the spaces above and around our world."[2] It is significant, too, that the word used to describe this kingdom in the air means thick and misty in contrast to bright and clear air![3] We see in the history of Job that the "prince of the power of the air" has authority to wield the forces of the air, for at his bidding lightning fell from heaven to consume the flocks of the faithful servant of God. It is significant also that when the Lord Jesus arose from His sleep in the storm on the lake He *rebuked* the winds and the sea—surely "the malignant spirits of air and water which had combined to excite the storm."[4] In relation to his attacks upon the children of men the prince of this world is called the "tempter" (1 Thes. 3:5), because it is his fiendish delight to tempt others from loyal obedience to God, as he once fell away himself! He is named "the devil" (1 Tim. 3:6-7)—a word *never used in the plural* and always and only of Satan himself. "The Hebrew name Satan occurs in the New Testament thirty-five times interchangeably with the Greek *diabolos*, which is also used thirty-five times. The word *diabolos* signifies separator and slanderer,"[5] or "malignant accuser." Satan is the great separator, and he separates by slandering. He slanders God to man, and carries to God slanderous statements about His children, even as he charged Job with self-interest. He separated the race of men from God in Eden, and ever since he has been separating men from each other, with hatred, malice, envy and jealousy. Therefore when the veil is drawn aside from the unseen world in the Apocalypse, he is specially named as the "accuser of the brethren" (Rev. 12:10, mar.), who is cast down by Michael and his angels

from his place in the air and overcome by the redeemed on earth as they testify to the "blood of the
Lamb" (Rev. 12:11) and yield their lives to the death
of the cross.

In the same unveiling of the conflict in the unseen
realm, we find him also described as "The great
dragon," the "old serpent"—probably from the form
he took in Eden—and the "deceiver of the whole
inhabited earth."

That the adversary still has the kingdom of the
world under his rule is unmistakably seen in his
attack upon the Lord Jesus in the wilderness temptation. The Lord was led under the constraint of the
Holy Spirit into the wilderness to be "tempted of
the devil"; after other temptations, we read that the
devil showed Him "all the kingdoms of the inhabited earth in a moment of time. And the devil said
unto Him, *To Thee will I give all this authority,* and
the glory of them: for it has been delivered unto
me; and to whomsoever I will I give it. If Thou
therefore will worship before me, it shall all be
Thine" (Luke 4:5–7, mar.).

"Worship before me"! What a daring condition to
put to the Son of God. The fallen archangel is craving
for worship still, for did he not say before his fall,
"I will be like the Most High"?

The Son of God did not deny the extent of Satan's
claim to *"all the kingdoms of the inhabited earth,"*
and later the Lord plainly speaks of his *kingdom* in the
fallen race of men. When some charged Jesus with
casting out demons "by the prince of the demons,"
the Lord said, "If Satan is divided against himself,
how shall his kingdom stand?" (Luke 11:18). And
He adds that "the strong man fully armed guardeth

his own court," until "a Stronger than he" comes
upon him, and sets his captives free. "Deliver us
from the evil one" (Matt. 6:13), the Lord taught His
disciples to pray. In His High-Priestly prayer on
the eve of His crucifixion He prayed for them that
they might be kept *"from the evil one"* (John 17:15),
for none knew more than He the extent of his
power and his malignant hatred of all who escape
his rule.

The words of the Apostle John also emphasize
the universality of the rule of the prince of this
world, for he writes "the whole world lieth in the
evil one" (1 John 5:19)—it is sunk in the darkness
which is his sphere, and is under the rule of the
"world-rulers of this darkness" (Eph. 6:12). The Word
of God speaks with no uncertain sound in this vital
matter, but how unwilling men are to believe the
truth. The Scripture makes no distinction between
high and low, or between cultured and ignorant,
when it states that the "whole world"—heathen and
Christendom—lies "in" the realm of the evil one.

In Africa, China, India, and all other heathen
lands, the one whose spiritual senses have been
awakened is keenly conscious of the sovereignty of
the prince of darkness, for there the deceiver of the
whole inhabited earth is daring in his tyranny,
holding men and women in gross and open sin. In
civilized countries, where the people are more
Christianized, or are to a certain extent familiar
with the Scriptures, the god of this age must veil
his working, but his rule is just as real. In these last
days, however, he is beginning more openly to
manifest himself as the prince of the world. He
covets to be recognized and to usurp the place of

God in the world. Slowly he is familiarizing people with his name. Palmistry, clairvoyance, planchette, and other means of intercourse with the spirits of evil, are abounding and increasing on every hand. In fact, by every possible means the enemy of God is seeking outward recognition as the prince of this world, with all men subject to his power.

The adversary has not only his kingdom, but he has also his organized government, which the Apostle Paul describes as "Principalities. . . Powers. . . Sovereigns of this present darkness" (Eph. 6:12, CH), and glimpses of the hierarchy of evil are clearly given in many parts of sacred writ. We read of "Satan's throne," where "Satan dwelleth" (Rev. 2:13); of "his ministers" (2 Cor. 11:15); of his "principalities" and his "powers"; and of his hosts of "spirits of evil" (Eph. 6:12, CH) in the heavens. Daniel's account of his interview with the messenger from God also reveals that these principalities and powers of Satan are given charge of specified countries, for the satanic "Prince of Persia" withstood the heavenly messenger who said that on his return he would again have to meet with the same Prince, together with the "Prince of Greece" (Dan. 10:13, 20).

Satan therefore reigns over an aerial kingdom of hierarchies and spiritual powers, and a kingdom on earth in the world of men. And he governs by means of an organized government: "principalities" who rule over various lands; "powers" who are placed by him in positions of authority—angels of the devil (see Matt. 25:41), consisting of those who chose to follow him into sin when he rebelled against God; and the demons, who a vast majority of early Christian writers think are the spirits of the dead who bore a bad character in this life, and who now crave some relief from their restless existence by entering the bodies of men. We read that they even preferred to enter the bodies of swine, rather than be cast out into homeless wandering again or into the place they manifestly dreaded, called the abyss (Luke 8:31, 33). They are at any rate plainly described as wicked spirits who are under the complete command of Beelzebub their prince.

As we read, however, let us not forget that all these hosts of evil are compelled to acknowledge the Sovereign Lord of the Universe! *Unbelievers in God are alone to be found on earth,* for although the powers of evil deceive men and keep them in darkness and unbelief, they themselves "believe and shudder" (James 2:19), knowing that they are reserved unto judgment in the day of the Lord.

In his organized government the adversary has also a *religion* for those whom he can delude and deceive. He has methods of cultivating communion with himself, showing his perfect mimicry of the worship of the true God and His Son Jesus Christ.

In Paul's first letter to the Corinthians one aspect of Satan's religion is revealed as we are shown what *idol worship* actually means. The apostle explains that in itself, as wood, or stone, or metal, an idol is "nothing in the world," but he makes it unmistakably clear that the *demon* at the back of the wood and stone is an awful reality. He points out that sacrifices offered to idols are really *"sacrifices to demons."* Therefore they who would walk in fellowship with God must "flee from idolatry," lest they would hold *"communion with demons."* They dare not take the "cup of the Lord" and the "cup of demons," partake of the "table of the Lord" and of the "table of demons" (1 Cor. 10:19–22, CH). This matter was vital to the Corinthians, as it now is to Christians in heathen lands, for often the meat offered for sale in the marketplace was meat which had first been offered to idols. Some of the Corinthian Christians had accepted invitations to feasts celebrated in the temple of heathen gods—feasts which were acts of idolatrous worship. But the apostle knew that the spirit forces behind the outward idol worship were very real, and so he urges that not in the remotest way must the child of God have *contact with the powers of darkness* through these things—even to please their friends, or because the idol itself means nothing in the world to them.

We see how deeply the fallen archangel has revolted from his allegiance to the Most High God, for he not only deceives, and tempts, and holds in darkness the human race, but he adds to their destruction and deepens his hold upon souls. He does this by seeking to meet the desire for an object of worship which lies dormant in every breast—for man was created for God, and even in his fallen condition he retains the consciousness of a higher power and the instinct to worship and adore.

Apart from direct satanic worship as manifested among the heathen in their bowing down to idols, Satan has other ways of meeting the need for some religion which is part of the instinct of men. The Apostle Paul writes to the Romans, "Thou that abhorrest idols, dost thou commit sacrilege?" (Rom. 2:22, mar.) as he shows that no outward rite or ceremonial fulfillment of the law is acceptable to God apart from the putting away of sin, and the seeking of God in spirit and in truth (Rom. 2:28–29). Satan knows this and therefore persuades men that outward obedience to some creed is enough. He thus deludes multitudes into a false peace by causing them to rest upon an outward form of words or ceremony, while inwardly he keeps them under the darkness of his rule.

In the Lord's message to the church at Smyrna He spoke of those who "*say* they are Jews, and they are not, but are a synagogue of Satan" (Rev. 2:9). It appears by this that the adversary has not only a religion which gives him worship through material images, but that his "synagogue"—or congregation— is made up of professors of religion who are without the inward truth. The Apostle John uses plain language concerning this when he writes, "If we *say* that we have fellowship with Him, and walk in darkness [*i.e.*, in sin], we lie, and do not the truth" (1 John 1:6, KJV). And the most severe words that ever passed the lips of the Lord Christ when on earth were His scathing exposures of the Pharisees. "They *say* and do not" He said, and "outwardly appear righteous unto men," when inwardly full of hypocrisy. He told them their actual condition, saying that they were of their "father the devil"; He called them "serpents," and the "offspring of vipers," saying that every proselyte they gained was made more a "son of hell" than themselves (Matt. 23:15)! And yet the Pharisees claimed *God as their Father*, and were of the straitest sect in Israel in the outward fulfilling of the law! The Lord's strong words against the professors of "godliness without the power thereof"—the divine energy which saves from sin—makes it therefore appear that Satan's invisible "church" is filled. Filled not with the openly sinful, nor the purely ignorant, but with those who make religion a cloak while they are really subjects of Satan, obeying his will, and serving him all the time, as "all their works they do for to be seen of men."

The worship of idols and the hypocritical profession of godliness without the inward reality are not the only aspects of Satan's religion—for in both of these men are often unconscious of their condition and would be startled if they knew the truth. The archenemy desires to have greater possession of human beings than this and craves the open recognition of his power and authority with the *deliberate surrender* of the will to him. To obtain this, the apostle says, Satan can fashion himself as an "angel of light" (2 Cor. 11:14), to allure those he desires to win for his particular use. Probably the fallen archangel has not lost the form of wondrous beauty in which he was created, but only the light of God has gone out of him and darkness fills his whole being—and this he can veil when occasion demands and he desires to counterfeit the angels of God. His reward is great to all who will openly acknowledge him, and he has his "deep things" to reveal to those who will fully yield to him.

The Lord refers to these "deep things of Satan" (Rev. 2:24) in His message to the church at Thyatira. The Apostle Paul wrote to Timothy that the Holy Spirit had expressly told him that in the latter days the adversary would seek to draw many away from faith in Christ by the teaching of spirits inculcating "doctrines of demons" (1 Tim. 4:1). Satan has "doctrines" as well as a system of worship—a "cup," a "table," and a "synagogue"! The character of the instrument usable by the spirits should be noted, for Paul said that the teaching would be given through men who would *profess to be what they were not,* and whose consciences would be seared as with a hot iron—for only thus could they be incapable of feeling the sinfulness of sin and be reckless concerning the awful judgment which must come on all who wreck the souls of others as well as their own.

These "teachings of demons," through false teachers acting under their control, had already begun in the first century, and seducing spirits were evidently at work in the church at Thyatira drawing servants of God from their Lord into the "deep things of Satan." One calling herself a prophetess was leading souls astray, teaching them to "eat things sacrificed to idols" which, we have already noticed, was so strongly forbidden by Paul. The apostle knew that they who did this were laying themselves open to the inroad of satanic power by having contact with the wicked spirits behind the idol; every idolator practically had fellowship with demons. The Lord's complaint was that the church allowed these things to be in its midst—things upon which He pronounced the most awful warning of certain judgment.

Let the children of God take heed, for traces of the subtle teaching of seducing spirits are sometimes discernible among groups of believers who seek to press on into the "deep things of God," and do not know the devices of the adversary. But we shall refer to this later on, and will only point out here that Satan's religion—however diverse in manifestation and name—always has one clearly defined mark in the *omission of the gospel of Calvary.* And by this test all "gospels" that are not *the* gospel may be recognized! The omission includes: the atoning death of the Son of God; His propitiation for sin; His blotting out of sin; His deliverance from the power of sin and the flesh by the severing power of the cross; His call of the blood-redeemed soul to the cross in humiliation of self, and sacrifice for others. In brief, all that Calvary means is emphatically repudiated, or else carefully omitted, in the doctrines of the seducing spirits which are evolved in hell! Let everyone thus test the tenets of Theosophy, of Christian Science, and the other teachings now being poured into the world by spirits of evil, who do not hesitate to appropiate for their purposes the very language describing the effects and blessings of the gospel. Peace, joy, love, sacrifice, yes, and even righteousness (as far as outward right-doing is meant), are now included in Satan's doctrines, devised to deceive, if possible, the very elect. These apparent "fruits of the Spirit" are not of the Holy Spirit unless the cross is accepted in its crucifying power. "That which is born of the flesh is *flesh*," said the Lord, though it be dressed in garments of peace and love and joy; and he that sows to the flesh must "of the flesh reap corruption," however beautiful it may appear outwardly. The aim of the adversary is: to retain the "flesh" in its full strength; to glorify the "flesh" even in the way of "righteousness"; to please the "flesh" in giving it the comfort of peace and joy and happiness; to allure the flesh by promise of escape from pain and suffering. But this "gospel" is the exact opposite of the gospel of Calvary, which brings the flesh to the cross, shows its inability to

produce the true righteousness which is acceptable
to God, and reveals the selfishness of ever craving
for peace and joy, and the self-indulgence of desiring to escape all the suffering which lies in the path
of fellowship with the Lamb of God. Of the still
more subtle attempts of teaching demons to lead
souls into sin, and sinful indulgence of the flesh
under the delusion of fellowship with God, we cannot speak. The words of the Lord to the church at
Thyatira show where the deep things of Satan lead.

It cannot be said that there is no *mention* of the
cross in Satan's religious teaching, but it is the cross
as only an *outward symbol* without the inward power;
Satan knows that it is only the real acceptance of
the death of Christ—or cross of Christ—which
saves from sin. There is no truth of God that the
fallen archangel, who was once full of wisdom, has
not counterfeited and used against his Creator.
Even the cross, where he was conquered by the
Prince of Life, he has made a symbol and used it as
a weapon against his Conqueror. There are cities
almost wholly under his sway today, above which
there glitter upon golden domes many symbols of
the cross—cities where the darkness of this world
resting on the people is a darkness to be felt, for sin
and wickedness reign supreme.

A messenger of the cross once drove along a
street in one such city, and while gazing at the
innumerable crosses standing out against the
brilliant blue sky there suddenly rang out in
his ears a hideous satanic laugh, indescribably
mocking, as the evil one cried, "I have taken
the symbol of my conquest and have used it
against my Conqueror." Under the "sign of the

cross," multitudes can be under the sway and in the power of the archenemy of God.

Notes

[1] Rev. Andrew Murray.
[2] Seiss.
[3] Pember.
[4] ibid.
[5] Blackstone.

CHAPTER THREE

The adversary's subjects on the inhabited earth. How he retains his kingdom and control in the world of men.

"THE whole world lieth in the evil one," declares the Apostle John, but it is of the supremest importance to the prince of this world that those who dwell in his realm should not know it. Therefore he exerts all his ingenuity to keep them unconscious of their condition. Again the Scriptures of truth give light upon this aspect of the adversary's working.

To keep men ignorant of their position *he blinds their minds!* "The god of this world hath blinded the minds [mar., thoughts] of the unbelieving, that the light of the gospel . . . should not dawn upon them" (2 Cor. 4:4). The adversary dreads the light of God, for light reveals things as they are, both in the natural and the spiritual world. "Ye shall know the truth, and the truth shall make you free," said the Lord Jesus (John 8:32). The truth about the love of God to men, of men as sinners needing a Saviour, and of God's gift of a perfect Saviour, able to save from sin and deliver from the captivity of the devil,

when really apprehended by the soul—must set free.
So the adversary hides the truth from his captives.
They are kept "darkened in their understanding,"
and are thus "alienated from the life of God because of the ignorance that is in them" (Eph. 4:18).

The Lord's words—that the good ground which
received the seed was in the one "that heareth the
word, and *understandeth* it" (Matt. 13:23)—evidence
the fact that the truth must reach the *understanding*
to be effectual in delivering the soul. Again the
Apostle Paul prays for the Colossians that they may
be given spiritual "understanding" (Col. 1:9), and John
says the Son of God *"hath given us an understanding,
that we know Him that is true"* (1 John 5:20). The
adversary therefore labors to keep the understanding
darkened, blinding the mind with (1) wrong thoughts
about God, (2) prejudices of all kinds, (3) the phi-
losophies of earth, (4) false reasonings concerning
spiritual things; or else he occupies the thoughts
with earthly things—earthly idols or the cares and
pleasures of this life.

It is important that we recognize the adversary at
the back of all these things if we are to be effectual
instruments in the hand of God for the translating of
souls out of the power of darkness into the Kingdom
of God's dear Son. The Spirit of God alone can defeat
the evil one and destroy the veil which darkens
men's minds. So *the power of the blood of Jesus* must
be claimed to act upon the satanic force *behind the
darkened understanding,* as we watch unto prayer for
the words of truth to be given by the Spirit—truth
which will deliver the captive from his bonds.

The adversary works in men without their knowledge.
"Ye once walked according to the course of this

world, according to the prince of the powers of the air, of the spirit that now worketh in the sons of disobedience" (Eph. 2:2). The Scriptures always unveil the *source* or cause of things which are seen! The apostle writes that men who walk according to the thoughts of this world are controlled by the prince of this world; he is *the spirit working in them* as they do the "desires of the flesh," and of their own thoughts. They are therefore "children of wrath" by nature and by action! But they do not know that the prince of the powers of the air is working in them, behind and through the flesh, and in their darkened mind—thus the adversary retains his hold. "Let them please themselves," he cries, "let them fulfill the desires of the flesh, and of their thoughts, and they will remain like myself, 'sons of disobedience.'"

The adversary seeks to snatch away the word of truth. "When anyone heareth the word . . . and understandeth it not, then cometh the evil one, and snatcheth away . . . " (Matt. 13:19). The adversary or his minions attend every preaching of the word of truth, and when the word does not enter the understanding it is easily snatched away—the thought is that of a bird snatching ravenously seed fallen on a hard pathway. Once the smallest seed of the word of truth enters the understanding it cannot be dislodged; it is sure to bring forth fruit in its season, unless it is choked by other things entering in. What multitudes hear the word and "understanding it not" pass on their way, still remaining in the realm of the evil one!

The adversary keeps his subjects in a false peace. "The strong man fully armed guardeth his own

court," and "his goods are in peace" (Luke 11:21).
The context of this passage shows the strong man
to be the devil; and here the adversary is pictured
as in full control of the darkened sinner, keeping
him in peace, wholly unaware of his condition, and
guarded carefully by the terrible one who is "fully
armed" to meet every attempt to deliver the captive from his bonds. How often a man resents his
peace being disturbed and cries again and again, "Let
me alone," until at last the Strong One of Calvary
conquers the strong man and sets the captive free.

*Again the adversary often incites opposition to the
truth.* The apostles knew the satanic forces they were
in conflict with, and so Paul wrote to Timothy concerning "them that oppose"—counseling instruction
with *meekness,* so that they might return to sober-
ness "out of the snare of the devil" (2 Tim. 2:25–26,
mar.). When the soul is roused enough to oppose, its
deliverance is most likely near at hand, as it was
with Saul of Tarsus. Never look at the opposing
man, but at the snare of the devil around him; be
gentle, forbearing and apt to teach, so that you may
deliver him from the captivity of the evil one.

But the time comes when the "Stronger than
he"—the Man of Calvary—lays hold of the captive
soul, and he is delivered "out of the power of darkness, and translated . . . into the Kingdom of the
Son" (Col. 1:13). What are the adversary's fresh
tactics now? The seed of the truth has entered the
understanding of the captive and he is set free to
proclaim the truth to others, to take the prey from
the mighty. But now the deceiver sets to work, and—

The adversary counterfeits the true work of God.
"While men slept, his enemy came and sowed tares

also among the wheat." The "tares are the sons of
the evil one . . . the enemy that sowed them is the
devil" (Matt. 13:25, 38–39). The true seed has taken
root and is growing and ripening for the heavenly
garner—but the adversary determines to nullify or
destroy the witness of the delivered ones. He scatters
among the growing wheat the tares, which the Lord
plainly explains to be "the sons of the evil one." *The
attention of the world will be drawn to the counterfeits*
and the true living seed of God remains hidden, for
the tares look like the wheat until the time for fruit!
And God looks on! "Let both grow together till the
harvest," He decrees, for the tares cannot be uprooted
without danger to the growing wheat. The adversary also works on! The Lord's wheat and the
adversary's tares, the true and the counterfeit, are
always found side by side throughout the inhabited earth—the Christ and His foe each seeking
possession of the children of men.

Before we go further let us pause here and face the
fact that the Scriptures declare these things to be true
concerning all men, whether they are high or low,
rich or poor, cultured or ignorant. There is no trace
given of neutral ground. "There is no distinction" of
race, "no respect of persons with God" (Rom. 2:11),
no qualification of great or small sins. "The Scripture hath shut up all under sin" (Gal. 3:22), "that
every mouth may be stopped, and all the world
may become guilty before God" (Rom. 3:19, KJV).
"He that doeth sin is of the devil; for the devil
sinneth from the beginning" (1 John 3:8), writes the
Apostle John in emphatic language. The divine life
which comes from God and is implanted in the
child of God does not sin, for the good tree bears

good fruit. The fallen life must also bring forth its own fruit of sin. This may be sin in greater or lesser degree, it is true, but it is sin as God sees sin.

The apostle furthermore declares that by their fruits "the children of God are manifest, and the children of the devil" (1 John 3:10). The supreme test is *fruit*. Love to others and righteousness of life are fruits of the true life of God, and they who are begotten of God manifest such fruits. They do not, as in their former condition, practice sin as a habit, although they may yield to and fall into sin even after they become children of God.

We have already referred to the Lord's words to the Pharisees, but here we note again how they show that outward profession of religion and the most exact obedience to ceremonial law may leave a soul unchanged in the *source* of its inner life. "Ye are of your father the devil," said the Lord to the Pharisees, who belonged to the strictest religious sect of their day and claimed God to be their Father. How sharply the line is drawn! How the word of truth pierces to the very joints and marrow of the inner man and lays bare the source of the life. *We are children of the one by whose life we live.* Children of God if His life is imparted to us, or "children of the devil" if we live under his control, doing the desires of the flesh and of the mind—children of wrath, even as others.

The adversary has not yet brought into action all the means by which he holds his subjects under his power when he simply blinds their minds, hides behind the fulfilling of their own thoughts and the desires of the flesh, snatches away every seed of truth, keeps them in a false peace, incites them to oppose the truth, or otherwise seeks to nullify the witness of those who are delivered from his power—such as by counterfeiting the true and drawing the attention of the blinded world to his counterfeits. Beyond all this the prince of this world seeks to obtain the entire possession and control of men as his special instruments, willing intelligently to fulfill his will and carry out his plans—just as in the Kingdom of God there are some who are fully abandoned to God, to be possessed and filled by the Holy Spirit for the extension of the Kingdom of Jesus Christ. The devil needs the voices and minds of men to reach other men, in the same way that the Spirit of God seeks to embody Himself in human beings to reach their fellows.

We have already noticed the unvarying proximity of the wheat and the tares, the true and the counterfeit, the working of God and the working of the devil side by side throughout the world; and we may expect towards the end of the age a greater manifestation of both in all directions. The devil will meet the supernatural workings of God with his "power and signs and lying wonders" (2 Thess. 2:9), until the Antichrist is fully revealed and the Bride of Christ is taken to the throne of the heavenly Bridegroom.

The archfiend has studied the fallen race of Adam for many thousands of years and knows how to allure his subjects. They who are grossly flesh he gives up to the desires of the flesh, "unclean spirits" often entering the bodies of men as in the days of old. But among the sons of men there are some with more spirit capacity than others; these the prince of darkness deludes in another way, for they are the ones especially open to his snares and most likely to become his tools to work out his will. These souls would not be allured by the "flesh," nor would vain philosophy and reasonings charm them. Beguiled, as the serpent beguiled Eve, by the fascination of the knowledge of good and evil, they are drawn into unlawful dealings with the spirit world, until some are given "a spirit of divination," like the damsel at Philippi (Acts 16:16), or are led into "magical arts," like Simon the sorcerer in the days of Paul.

Such are the workings of the adversary today in spritism, palmistry, crystal-gazing and such. Men and women again are dealing with familiar spirits and seeking on behalf of the living unto the dead. In the twentieth century, in the face of an open Bible and the light of the gospel, professed "Christian people" once more are practicing the "abominations" which caused the Lord to cast out the nations of Canaan before His people Israel. These abominations Jehovah solemnly forbade Israel to touch, saying, "When thou art come into the land . . . there shall not be found with thee . . . one that useth divination, one that practiceth augury, or an enchanter, or a sorcerer, or a charmer, or a consulter with a familiar spirit, or a wizard, or a necromancer. For whosoever doeth these things is an abomination unto Jehovah" (Deut. 18:9–12).

Though faced with His words, Israel sinned against God in these things until He had to cast them out as He had done the nations before them. In Christendom, too, the archfiend is leading astray multitudes into the abominations—in England and America, as well as in Europe. But the Holy God has not changed! If He spared not Israel, whom He was pleased to make His peculiar people, neither will He fail to judge those who, with greater light and knowledge than even Israel had, sin against Him in these things.

All this is in fulfillment of the Apostle Paul's forecast of the latter days. As we have seen, even in his time "the mystery of iniquity" (2 Thess. 2:7, KJV) had begun to work, and it has gone on working down the centuries until now. It now seems that the prince of darkness is rapidly preparing the world for the revealing of the "lawless one," he "whose presence is according to the working of Satan with all power and signs and wonders of falsehood" (2 Thess. 2:9, mar.). They who will be ensnared by these lying wonders will be the ones who "received not the love of the truth, that they might be saved"—who "for this cause" were given up by God to "strong delusions" (2 Thess. 2:10–11, KJV) to believe a lie, and thus become open to judgment because they rejected His truth and had pleasure in unrighteousness.

The grievous times are upon us. Men are "lovers of self, lovers of money . . . lovers of pleasure rather than lovers of God; holding a form of godliness" while denying the power thereof. Of this character are they, writes the apostle, who "creep into houses, and take captive silly women laden with sins," women led away by their own desires, "ever learning, and never able to come to the knowledge of the truth" (2 Tim. 3:1–6). Many indeed are thus led away by a *form* of godliness, and do not know the power thereof—souls laden with sins, yet unable to apprehend the power of the gospel of Calvary.

CHAPTER FOUR

*How the adversary was conquered at Calvary.
The proclamation of the conquest throughout
his dominions.*

L ET us now see how God planned to deliver the
earth from the power of the fallen archangel.
The first promise of deliverance was made in Eden,
after Satan had beguiled the woman and brought
about the downfall of the human race. The Lord
God pronounced a curse upon the serpent and then
promised to the woman a Seed which would bruise
his head (Gen. 3:14–15).

This Seed was the Son of God, for "when the
fullness of time came, God sent forth His Son, born
of a woman, born under the law, that He might
redeem them which were under the law" (Gal. 4:4–5).
Who, "existing in the form of God, counted not the
being on an equality with God a thing to be grasped,
but emptied Himself . . . becoming in the likeness
of men" (Phil. 2:6–7, mar.), so that, as the Second
Adam, He might perfectly obey God and finally
offer Himself as a propitiation for the sins of the
fallen race. As the Representative Man He would
die on the cross of Calvary, bring to an end the

fallen race in His own person, and create in Himself—born out of His death on the cross—a new race of sons of God, a "new creation" after His own likeness. Thus He would bring to nought the devil and deliver his ruined subjects by the weapon of death—the very result of sin.

That all hell was moved over His incarnation we may be sure; and the prince of darkness prompted Herod the king to slay innocent little ones, in the hope of destroying Him who had come to earth to bring the prince of the world to an end of his reign.

When the God-man reached the age of thirty, He came out of His retirement to carry through the plan devised in the far-back ages of eternity for the redemption of the world. He at once identified Himself, sinless Being though He was, with the sinners He had come to save. He entered the Jordan where they were being baptized, confessing their sins. He was anointed with the Spirit of God and acknowledged by His Father in a voice from heaven, and then was led by the Spirit into the wilderness to meet the direct attack of His foe. Analagous to the garden where the first Adam fell, the Second Adam was for forty days alone in the midst of wild beasts. The prince of darkness pressed upon Him and sought by every means to persuade Him to listen to his voice. He sought to tempt Him through His human nature and its hunger, but the Lord would not supply His own need before His Father's time; he gave Him a vision of the world and offered it to Him for one act of submission; he urged upon Him the presumptuous testing of His Father's protection. But to every suggestion the God-man made reply, *"It is written."* Eve listened to the devil's "Hath God said?" but the Second Adam refused all temptation with the words "God *hath* said," thus foiling the foe. "And when the devil had completed every temptation, he departed from Him for a season" (Luke 4:13).

From the wilderness the Son of God came forth victorious to find the adversary meeting Him again, but this time by his wicked spirits in possession of men. He went to Galilee, and there in the synagogue itself was a man with "the spirit of an unclean demon." Quickly the demon recognized the Christ and cried out, "I know Thee who Thou art, the Holy One of God!" (Luke 4:33–34). The prince of the demons had been conquered in the long conflict in the wilderness, so now "with authority and power" the Son of God commanded the unclean spirits as He met them. They recognized Him, and "whensoever they beheld Him, fell down before Him, and cried, saying, Thou art the Son of God." A legion of demons—some six thousand of the minions of the prince of the aerial regions—held one poor soul, as he cried out, "What have I to do with Thee, Jesus, Thou Son of the Most High God? I beseech Thee, torment me not" (Luke 8:28–29).

The wicked spirits knew Him, and bore witness to Him as the Son of God, but "rebuking them, He suffered them not to speak, because they knew that He was the Christ." (Luke 4:41). He would not have the witness of evil spirits to enforce His claim upon men. The works which He did, and the words of life which He spoke, by the indwelling Presence of the Father and the sealing of the Holy Spirit, were sufficient to reveal to prepared hearts whence He came and who He was. He knew that all who would be taught of God would come to Him and acknowledge Him in truth to be the Christ, the Son of the living God.

Many today are seeking to know the spirit world through channels forbidden by God. They excuse themselves by saying that they desire to know the truth concerning the resurrection of the dead and the existence of another world. But we need to remember the attitude of the Lord to the witness of evil spirits, for He expressly said if men received not the testimony of "Moses and the prophets"—the written Scriptures of the Old Testament—neither would they be persuaded by any miracle, even if one rose from the dead. What need is there of any proof of spiritual truths except the witness of the Holy Spirit through the Scriptures? The trouble is this: the *Holy* Spirit reveals only to those who desire to part with sin, while the evil spirits reveal so as to *keep in sin* all who venture on forbidden ground in defiance of God's commands.

We have seen that the demons recognized the Christ and always acknowledged Him as having authority over them. But Satan, the prince of the demons, continued his attacks all the way to the cross. He left Jesus after the victory in the wilderness, but only "for a season." He approached Him again through His impulsive but devoted disciple Peter who, when he was told of the cross awaiting his Master, prayed Him to pity Himself and turn from such a path. This was not the only time that the adversary worked through Peter to grieve the Lord! Peter in his self-confidence gave advantage to the foe, who surely rejoiced over his fall into denying the Lord with curses and lies. "Satan obtained him" to "sift him as wheat" (Luke 22:31, mar.), and used him to bring about part of the very suffering of the path to the cross, which he had prayed the Lord to shun. The adversary also obtained an instrument in Judas through his covetousness and through him caused the Son of God untold sorrow and pain, until at last the prince of darkness was able to enter into him and use him as his tool to betray the Lord and bring about the cross. The devil had at first offered the kingdom of the world to the Christ without a cross; then he sought to turn Him from it by the lips of one of His disciples; and finally he entered into one of them[1] to lead Him to the cross, seeming to believe in his arrogance and pride that he could destroy by death the Son of the eternal God.

"This is your hour, and the power of darkness" (Luke 22:53), said the Lord Christ as He was seized in the garden of Gethsemane and led away to death. He knew what Calvary would mean! "For this cause came I unto this hour," He said to His disciples on the eve of His passion. "Now is the judgment of this world: now shall the prince of this world be cast out. And I, if I be lifted up from the earth, will draw men unto Myself. But this He said, signifying by what manner of death He should die" (John 12:27, 31–33). When the Son of God was lifted up from the earth on the cross of shame, in that very hour the power of darkness, the prince of this world, was judged; and by the wondrous power of the love manifested on Calvary's cross, men are drawn to the Son of God, won from allegiance to the archenemy of God and thus translated into the Kingdom of the Son of His love.

In His farewell words to His disciples, the Lord

told them that on His return to the Father He would send them the Spirit of Truth who would bear witness along with them—and convince the world of its sin of unbelief, of the gift of righteousness obtained for sinners, and of the judgment of the prince of the world. "Now shall the prince of this world be cast out," He said as He went to the cross; but after the cross the Spirit would testify "the prince of this world *hath been judged*" (John 16:11). The place of victory over the fallen archangel was therefore the

CROSS OF CALVARY.

The very cross by which the devil meant to end the life of the Son of God was his own undoing. On the cross the Prince of Life "stripped off from Himself principalities and powers," and "made a show of them openly, triumphing over them in it" (Col. 2:15).[2] The "weakness of God is stronger than men" (1 Cor. 1:25). The Christ was "crucified through weakness" (2 Cor. 13:4), and yet the prince of darkness, by putting Him to open shame before a mocking world, was himself, with all his principalities and powers, put to open shame before the heavenly hosts of God. The powers of darkness were "spoiled" and robbed of their prey, and triumphed over in the very hour which they had planned to be the hour of their own victory!

The work was accomplished! The disobedience of the first Adam was met by the obedience of the Second—the Lord from heaven. The sin, upon which must come the wages of death, had been atoned for by death, for the punishment of death was carried out upon the sinless One, who took upon Himself the sins of the world and died as the Representative Man. The fallen race of Adam,

which God had said must be "blotted out" (Gen.
6:7, mar.; 7:23, mar.) because "every imagination of
the thoughts of the heart was only evil continually," was nailed to the cross in the person of the
Second Adam. By the cross the Lord from heaven
triumphed over the prince of darkness! *"Through
death"*—the very result of sin; *"through death"*—the
very weapon by which the evil one held his subjects in bondage; *"through death"*—drinking the cup
of death to its dregs for the whole world; *"through
death"*—the Prince of Life *destroyed* "him that had
the power of death, that is, the devil" (Heb. 2:14)!
Satan has fallen from heaven. He is "cast out," his
power destroyed, his kingdom shaken, at the place
called Calvary!

Through the work accomplished on the cross,
"being put to death in the flesh," the Christ was
"made alive in the Spirit" (1 Pet. 3:18). God raised
Him up "having loosed the pangs of death: because it was not possible that He should be holden
of it" (Acts 2:24), and afterwards He ascended into
heaven and sat down in triumph at His Father's
right hand. As the Psalmist foretold: "Jehovah saith
unto my Lord, Sit Thou at My right hand, until I
make Thine enemies Thy footstool" (Ps. 110:1). "Being
therefore at the right hand of God exalted, and
having received of the Father the promise of the
Holy Spirit, He hath poured forth" (Acts 2:33, mar.)
the Spirit on the day of Pentecost—to anoint and
equip His prepared disciples for the express purpose of witnessing to Him as the Risen Saviour,
and proclaiming to the whole world lying in the
evil one the victory of Calvary. The work accomplished on the cross was a finished and full re-

demption. Atonement was made for the sins of the whole world, and the prince of the world was "cast out" potentially from his sovereignty over the world. But now the captives of sin and Satan must, one by one of their own free choice, accept the deliverance won for them on Calvary, for the sons of men retain by heritage the freedom of will given to their ancestors in the garden of Eden.

The Son of God could but come and give His life as a ransom, and conquer their spiritual foe. As Ascended Lord He could but send the Eternal Spirit to convince the captives of their need and the way to victory. On their part they must *choose* whom they would now serve! They must of their own free will elect to enter the Kingdom of their Redeemer and leave the sphere and service of their captor. Choosing the rule of the Conqueror of Calvary, by simple faith in Him they would be *united*, or grafted, into Him in His death on the cross and be delivered out of the power of darkness—translated into the realm of their Deliverer. The cross would thus be a gate through which they passed out of the sphere of darkness into the sphere of the marvelous light of God, for God is Light and in Him is no darkness at all.

But men being men, the Holy Spirit must embody Himself in men—to have men as His voices, men as His instruments, men as His object lessons—in order to win the sons of men. The proclamation of the conquest of the evil one, and liberty from his dominion, must be made by heralds all through his realm. On the day of Pentecost the souls prepared by Christ Himself were gathered together with one accord, waiting for the promised equipment from on high before going forth as heralds of the cross. And suddenly He came! The Eternal Spirit of the Father! The gift of the Son! And He filled the waiting souls through whom He would convince fallen men of the finished redemption at Calvary. All who obeyed His command and waited for the promise of the Father were sealed with fire from heaven and equipped with the power of the Spirit upon them to wield the all-prevailing name of the Conqueror from Calvary. The Glorified Lord Himself by His Spirit worked with them, "confirming the word by the signs that followed."

Their commission was *foreshadowed* by the Christ when He said to the seventy, "Behold, I have given you authority to tread upon serpents and scorpions, and over all the power of the enemy: and nothing shall in any wise hurt you" (Luke 10:19). Their commission was *confirmed* by Him after His resurrection, in the interval before He ascended into heaven, when He said, "These signs shall accompany them that believe: in My name shall they cast out demons" (Mark 16:17); also in the direct message from heaven of the Ascended Lord when He afterwards appeared to His herald Paul, and said, "To this end have I appeared unto thee, to appoint thee a minister and a witness . . . I send thee to open their eyes, to turn them from darkness to light and *from the power of Satan unto God*" (Acts 26:16–18, mar.).

In the account of the working of the Eternal Spirit through the apostles in the early days after Pentecost, we see how authority over the power of darkness was actually exercised by men equipped by the Holy Spirit, for under the ministry of Philip "unclean spirits, crying with loud voice, came out of many that were possessed with them" (Acts 8:7, KJV). On another occasion the Apostle Paul was troubled by a demon possessing a woman, who followed after the apostles, crying out that they were servants of the Most High God who proclaimed the way of salvation. Like the Lord, Paul did not want the testimony of evil spirits, so in calm assurance of the power of the name of the Conqueror, he spoke the word, "I charge thee in the name of Jesus Christ to come out of her." And it came out that very hour (Acts 16:16–18). Later the necessary condition of knowing the victory of Calvary *experientially* before the name of Jesus could have power over the adversary was emphasized when certain Jews who were exorcists took upon themselves to call the name of the Lord Jesus over those who had evil spirits, saying, "I adjure you by Jesus whom Paul preacheth." And the evil spirit answered and said unto them, "Jesus I recognize, and Paul I know; but who are ye?" And the man in whom the evil spirit was leaped on them, and overpowered them so that they fled naked and wounded (Acts 19:13–16). The all-conquering name of the Victor of Calvary needs the *Holy Spirit Himself to wield it* through men possessed by Him!

But the prince of this world has not been disposed to give up the kingdoms of the world without a struggle. We have seen how the history of the Church of Christ, down through two thousand years since the day of Pentecost, tells of the bitter fight of the conquered prince and shows that, although he was indeed judged at the cross, he is yet in possession of multitudes of men throughout the inhabited earth. But his time is getting short! Although he is still at large "going to and fro in the earth and walking up and down in it" (Job 1:7), holding men in his power and resisting to the utmost their obtaining knowledge of the victory won on Calvary's cross, his overthrow, and eventual casting into the bottomless pit, only awaits the gathering in of the last soul who elects to yield to the heavenly King.

The Most High God set a limit to the "day of grace" during which dispensation the tidings of the victory of Calvary had to be proclaimed throughout the earth. The enemy has sorely hindered the fulfillment of the commission committed to the Church of God. The adversary, disguised in men whom the Lord foretold to be "wolves in sheeps' clothing," has entered the flock. To cause divisions within the Church and deadly apathy has been his successful aim, with the sad result that men who know the story of Calvary have slept, and realm after realm of the enemy's dominion still lie in darkness and the shadow of death.

But the King never moves from His purpose. Though the enemy has hindered, and the Lord's children have slept, the word has been passed. "These good tidings of the Kingdom shall be preached in the whole inhabited earth for a testimony unto all the nations; and then shall the end come" (Matt. 24:14, mar.). With patient love the Lord has borne with His people, and in the latter days has awakened many of them to their commission—even devising means Himself to quickly send the message of His cross throughout the world. "The time is short!" He cries by His Spirit to His people. "Already it is time for you to awake out of sleep: for . . . the night is far spent, and the day is at hand" (Rom. 13:11–12). Meanwhile the attacks of the adversary upon the redeemed are turned by the all-wise Lord into the training and fitting of them for their great destiny in the coming reign of the Conqueror. The Victor of Calvary calls into one life with Himself all who accept His redemption, His cross, His Kingship and complete control. In the wondrous purpose of the grace of God, He determined to create through the death on Calvary a new race in the likeness of His Son, who would be "the firstborn among many brethren" (Rom. 8:29)— a new race which will reign with Him and, in the fullness of time, take the place of Satan and his angels in the government of the earth. The adversary is well aware of this purpose of the Most High God. Hence his bitter fight, for he knows the end that awaits him: when the angel of God comes down from heaven "having the key of the abyss, and a great chain in his hand," then he will lay hold on "the dragon, the old serpent, which is the Devil and Satan" (Rev. 20:1–2), and bind him for a thousand years, casting him into the abyss, shutting it and sealing it over him—finally afterwards to go into "the eternal fire which is prepared for the devil and his angels" (Matt. 25:41).

Notes

[1] We only read once of Satan himself entering a man, and this was Judas, for the work of betraying the Lord was too important to trust to any but himself. Dr. Pierson.

[2] Dr. Waller.

CHAPTER FIVE

The adversary's resistance to the liberation of his captives, and how souls are freed by the power of the cross.

WE have seen that the adversary has been conquered at Calvary and cast down from his throne of power, but is left at large while the proclamation of the victory is sent throughout his dominions for the purpose of giving the choice of masters to every human being. The adversary naturally resists to the utmost the work of the Holy Spirit in men as their eyes are opened to the truth, as one by one they accept the Redeemer as their Lord and King and are translated into His Kingdom. But far more keenly does the adversary resist the full enlightenment of the believer and his knowledge of the deepest meaning of Calvary. Satan knows it is this which sets the believer free from the false claims of the evil one and makes him so possessed by the Holy Spirit that he becomes an equipped and aggressive warrior in the army of the Lord, able by divine power to snatch the prey from the mighty in the name of the Victor of the cross.

Before we pass on to see how souls are liberated

by the message of Calvary, we must first briefly note
some of the ways in which the adversary resists our
full deliverance after the light of the gospel has
dawned on us and we have received the seed of the
Word into our hearts and realized the true peace of
the acceptance of the Saviour. The adversary knows
he has lost one of his subjects, but realizes that the
human will never cause much other loss to his kingdom if he can but retain some hold on him and
prevent him escaping entirely from his power. To
this end

He seeks to keep back the soul from full surrender to God.

> "Ananias, why hath *Satan* filled thy heart to de-
> ceive the Holy Spirit, and to keep back part . . . "
> (Acts 5:3, mar.).

It was at a time when many were placing themselves and their possessions entirely at the disposal
of the Lord, that Ananias looked on. He possibly
did not want to be singular, so not realizing the
character of the God he was trifling with he laid
part of his possessions at the apostles' feet, pre-
tending that it was his "all"! Peter, filled with the
Spirit, discerned the truth, and his stern words at
once unveil the source of the sin. *Satan* had "filled
his heart" to make him "keep back part." It would
have been better not to have offered at all, for God
only desires voluntary surrender and absolute honesty of purpose toward Himself.

"Truth in the inward parts" is necessary for realizing the deliverance offered by the Lord. An honest attitude toward God, an unreserved surrender
to Him with true purpose of heart, is required in
order to be His fully and forever. But "keep back

part," whispers the evil one, "for to yield all to God means to lose all."

But *"all for all"* it must be! Not because the Lord desires to take all away, but the "all" of Calvary's triumph is given on the condition of the surrender of "all" to Calvary's Victor. Because the "all" the Lord gives is from heaven and the "all" the soul resigns is of earth, "Keep back part for self" is therefore the tempter's whisper, as he enlarges upon the terrible consequences of committing all to God. Something kept for self gives place to the devil and keeps the Redeemer from His throne in the heart, and the full control of His Kingdom in the redeemed one.

He resists the removal of the filthy garments spotted by the flesh.

"Satan standing at his right hand to be his adversary" (Zech. 3:1).

This is an Old Testament picture of the attitude of the adversary to every soul who desires deliverance from his realm and rule, and admittance to the fellowship of God. Joshua the high priest is seen standing before the Lord clothed in filthy garments, with Satan as his adversary. Even so does the devil resist every child of God as he stands before the Lord seeking to be clothed with change of raiment. Clothed in the garments spotted by the flesh, the redeemed one stands in dumb helplessness before the Lord. The simple words "Jehovah rebuke thee, O Satan" are spoken, and the foe is silenced. He can only look on and see the grace of God as the command is given to those who stand by to take the filthy garments away. The iniquity is caused to pass away, and the soul is clothed in the righteousness of God and given a place of access to the Presence of the King. The soul seeking deliverance is here shown the way of victory over the adversary! We must not contend with him ourselves, but just as we are, stand before the Lord in our deep need and let Him rebuke the evil one. The work is then done for us, as we cease from our own efforts, letting God work and apply to us the power of Calvary.

He uses others to tempt us from the way of the cross.

> "Peter took Him, and began to rebuke Him, saying, Pity Thyself, Lord. . . . But He turned and said unto Peter, Get thee behind Me *Satan*: thou art a stumbling-block unto Me" (Matt. 16:22–23, KJV, mar.).

When the soul has yielded all in full surrender, and in dumb helplessness ceased from his own works to let God work in him, he knows by the Holy Spirit that he must take the cross and deny himself, if Christ is to see of the travail of His soul and be satisfied. But "Pity thyself" cries the adversary through the lips even of servants of God, who have dimmer vision of the things of God and do not know the eternal loss to the soul who listens to their plea.

"Pity thyself," the enemy whispers again and again, as the Holy Spirit detaches the soul from the things of earth to give it the gold of heaven. But "Get thee behind me, Satan" the redeemed one must cry as he looks behind the human voice, sees the adversary of God and determines by the grace of God to take up his cross and follow after his Lord to Calvary.

He inflames the life of nature into division and strife.

> "If ye have bitter jealousy and faction in your heart [it] is earthly, sensual, devilish" (Jam. 3:14–15).

The Apostle James uses very strong words in this passage, as he points out that all jealousy and faction has its source in the life which he calls "sensual" and "devilish"! Satan is shown here to be the real power working through the fallen life of nature.

When the believer has pressed on, and taken the cross, he will surely come face to face with something in his path which will arouse to its depth the life of nature. Possibly, when he has taken the cross for himself and consented to a path of self-effacement, circumstances arise when "loyalty demands that he should stand up for a friend"! The spirit of faction comes in, or jealousy for others, and the adversary triumphs. The apostle says that the wisdom that is from above is "without partiality." Oh that the children of God would take the words to heart and remember that all *division,* all *faction,* all *jealousy* for the "own" in friends, or denomination, is instigated by the evil one *to keep the believer in the sphere* lying under his rule—and consequently unable to wield over him the authority of heaven!

These are but a few of the devices of the prince of darkness to keep back the soul from the full deliverance of the cross. This calls for full surrender to God and absolute honesty of purpose; a ceasing from self-effort and a standing before the Lord in dumb acknowledgment of need; a taking of the path of the cross and refusal to pity self; a turning from the faction and divisions of earth—all this there must be if the soul is to know the victory of Calvary and enter into the life of overcoming on the throne.

But let us now go to Calvary, consider what it means, and see how souls are actually translated out of the realm of darkness into the sphere of light, in the Kingdom of God's dear Son.

We will think of the cross as a "gate" between the earthly realm of Satan and the heavenly sphere of life in Christ Jesus.

THE SPHERE OF   THE SPHERE OF
SATAN   CHRIST

But how are the captives of Satan to pass through the gate of the cross? They cannot do this of themselves, for no man can lift himself out of the horrible pit of sin. There is complete provision to meet the need! The Lord Jesus Christ not only died on the cross, not only offered Himself as a propitiation for sin, not only conquered the adversary there, but when He ascended into heaven and sat down on the right hand of the Majesty on High He received of His Father the gift of the Holy Spirit, whom He sent forth to bear witness to Him—to take of the things of Christ and reveal them to all who seek Him. It is the special office of the Eternal Spirit to reveal Christ to seeking souls; to breath into them the new life of God; to lead them into the apprehension of the truth—the truth which will make them free—and to apply to them the separating and delivering power of the death of Christ, as they accept and appropriate deliverance. Assuming therefore the captive is conscious of his need and desirous of deliverance, the Holy Spirit unveils the death of Christ first—

In relation to sin.

"His own self bare our sins in His body upon the

tree, that we, having died unto sins, might live
unto righteousness, by whose stripes ye were
healed" (1 Pet. 2:24).

The soul, under the burden and in the bondage
of sin, comes to Calvary where the Holy Spirit unveils to his wondering gaze the Prince of Glory
hanging upon the tree, becoming a curse for all
who were accursed under the curse of sin. As the
individual believes the Word of God and accepts
the Saviour, the Spirit at once applies the power of
the blood, and he obtains "peace through the blood
of the cross." The burden of sin passes away and
the Spirit bears witness to his spirit that he is a
reconciled child of God, being born of the Spirit,
who imparts to him the gift of life—new life, the
very life of the Son of God.

But the words of the Apostle Peter also show
that the sinner and the Saviour were one in the
sight of God as the Redeemer hung upon His cross.
The apostle says that He bore our sins on the tree,
"that we having died unto sins might live unto
righteousness"! It was the sinner who died when
the Substitute died! Died in Him to the sins which
He bore for him! It could never be that He bore our
sins, and died for us, purely that He might forgive
us our sins and leave us still under their power,
and hence under the power of Satan! The words of
the apostle make it quite plain that He bore our
sins on the tree so that in Him we should die to
them—or be delivered from them—and henceforth
live a new life "unto righteousness"; for by His
stripes we are healed from our sin-stricken condition and set free to live only unto God.

"To this end was the Son of God manifested, that

He might destroy the works of the devil" (1 John 3:8). The adversary holds his captives in his realm by keeping them under the bondage of a guilty conscience over the sins of their past or the power of present sin. But when the sinner sees that the Lord bore his sins on the tree, and *took the sinner there also,* the first ground is taken from the devil, for the Spirit takes possession of the redeemed one and reveals the Living Christ dwelling in the heart by faith. "Crucified" is His message to the liberated one—"Crucified with Him . . . no longer be in bondage to sin" (Rom. 6:6).

But there are few to whom the full gospel message comes at once so clearly! To many the first light is simply the forgiveness of past sin, as they apprehend the word of the Lord that "the Lord hath laid on Him the iniquity of us all," and "He that believeth *hath* everlasting life." But when this is so, the need of deliverance from the *bonds,* as well as the *guilt* of sin, is certain to press upon the pardoned sinner sooner or later—often through the bitterness of realizing the truth of the Master's words, "Every one that committeth sin is the bond-servant [or slave] of sin" (John 8:34).

When the soul learns the meaning of the cross in deliverance from the bondage of sin, whether it be at the time of conversion as it was at Pentecost, or later in what has been described as a "second blessing," it then enters upon the first stage of the overcoming life and upon a path of victory it never knew before. The cross is the gate into a life of liberty from the power of sin.

The cross and the works of the flesh.

"They that are of Christ Jesus have crucified the

flesh with the passions and the lusts thereof" (Gal. 5:24).

Here we come to Calvary and see the death of the Saviour dealing with the passions and desires of the flesh as well as the bondage of sin. We have already seen that the adversary keeps his subjects in his power by simply working in them to fulfill the desires of the flesh. But the Saviour carried the sinner to the cross in His own person, and as the redeemed soul apprehends this he finds the power of the cross acts as a circumcising knife to the flesh. Therefore, the apostle says, *"they that are of Christ Jesus"*—united to Him in His Risen life—*"have crucified* the flesh"—have been to Calvary and yielded to the cross the flesh, to be kept crucified there by the power of the Spirit of God day by day.

The believer has already apprehended death with Christ to the sins He has blotted out in His precious blood, and the Holy Spirit is already in possession of the redeemed one to cause him to live unto righteousness. But "the desire of the flesh fights against the Spirit, and the desire of the Spirit fights against the flesh" (Gal. 5:17, CH), for "these are contrary the one to the other." The "Spirit which He made to dwell in us yearneth even unto jealous envy" (Jam. 4:5, mar.). It is His work to bring the flesh to the cross, but He needs, on the part of the one He indwells, the whole will set on His side and complete trust in Him to do His work, as well as implicit obedience to His rule. The cross of Calvary is the triumphing power. "They that are of Christ Jesus have crucified the flesh" must be the continual faith of the soul, as "by the Spirit" he "makes to die the doings of the body" (Rom. 8:13, mar.)

and finds the Holy Spirit bears witness to the cross. This steadfast appropriation of the deliverance of death with Christ on the cross, in dependence on the co-working of the Divine Spirit, is even more necessary when the Holy Spirit begins to reveal to the soul more and more of the depths of the fallen life of Adam, against which He has waged war from generation to generation (Ex. 17:14, 16).

The word "flesh" used in Scripture seems to cover a very wide range, and to narrow it down into less than the meaning of the Word of God will limit our experience of the deliverance of the cross and rob us of the fullest life in God. The list of the recorded "works of the flesh" includes not only the grossest sins in the physical realm but sins directly *satanically* spiritual, such as "idolatry" and "sorcery," as well as sins of the heart and disposition such as "enmity, strife, jealousies, wraths, factions, *divisions*, and *parties*" (Gal. 5:19–21)! When all the grosser side has been dealt with in the life of the Christian, have "emulation," "variance," "strife," "factions," "divisions" over religious views, and also over the teaching of "holiness," no place among the consecrated people of God—even among those who have really apprehended deliverance from the bondage of sin and are truly indwelt by the Spirit of God? Unfortunately, very often they do. In practical experience it is therefore true that although the soul may see in one moment death to sin with Christ on the cross, and gladly and joyfully realize freedom from the bonds of sin, yet the indwelling Spirit of God must work deeper and deeper into the life, revealing the "flesh" in its ever-widening range and in every degree of its subtle working—even when it looks sanctified and is dressed in the garb of holiness. Then as the Spirit reveals, the believer must ever turn to Calvary with the definite faith that "they that are Christ's have crucified the flesh" and cast himself upon the Spirit of God to enable him to walk step by step "in the Spirit," not fulfilling the desires of the flesh. "Led by the Spirit," the fruit of the Spirit will then be manifested and ripen day by day to the glory of God—the precious fruits of "love, joy, peace, longsuffering, kindness, goodness, trustfulness, gentleness, and self-control" (Gal. 5:22–23, CH and ASV, mar.).

But is there no fight? Yes—but after the will is surrendered, and kept on the Lord's side in every hour of temptation, it is conflict between the Holy Spirit, in His strong desire to conquer the flesh, and the flesh, in its innate involuntary resistance to being conquered! The deciding factor is the *will* of the surrendered believer. *"To whom ye yield* yourselves, his servants ye are,"* writes the Apostle Paul to the Romans. If the redeemed one persistently asserts his position as crucified with Christ, and affirms continuously that "they that are of Christ Jesus *have* crucified the flesh," *refusing* at the same time to heed its demands, the Holy Spirit brings to bear the victory of Calvary upon the "works of the flesh," and crucifixion with Christ becomes experientially true. Thus does the believer become a victor over sin and over the life "after the flesh," which the adversary seeks by all means to nourish and retain, knowing that if it is continuously yielded to the cross, the redeemed one escapes from his power.

The cross and this present evil world.

"Our Lord Jesus Christ . . . gave Himself for our

sins, that He might deliver us out of this present
evil world" (Gal. 1:3–4).
"The cross of our Lord Jesus Christ, through which
the world hath been crucified unto me, and I unto
the world" (Gal. 6:14).

Another stage of the overcoming life meets us
here. Through the cross we have deliverance from
the power of sin, deliverance from the works of the
flesh, and now deliverance from the world which
lies in the evil one. Once again deliverance is clearly
shown to be by the apprehension of the death of
the sinner with the Saviour. By His cross, nailed
there with Him, the world is crucified to me. It is a
dead thing with which I have nothing to do. I am
henceforth "not of the world," but a citizen of
heaven. It is not only crucified to me, but I am
crucified to the world. I am no longer of any account in the world, or to the world. The gulf of
death has been fixed between us. I have left the
world in spirit and passed to the other world
through the gate of the cross, even as I shall finally
leave it when this mortal shall put on immortality.

The context of the chapter in which we find
Galatians 6:14 shows that Paul includes not only
the world lying in the evil one and separated from
God, but the *religious* world—insofar as the elements
of the world are in it. How subtle this "world" is
we all know! Its main characteristic is seen in the
desire to escape the cross and make a "fair show in
the flesh" (Gal. 6:12). This worldly attitude reveals
itself in the desire to be a success in the eyes of the
religious world—and in thousands of ways needs the
ceaseless light of the Spirit to reveal its snare. The
Apostle James refers to this attitude when he men-

tions the giving place to wealth and position in the very assembly gathered to worship God, with whom there is no respect of persons; and Paul when he points out the "philosophy and vain deceit, after the tradition of men," which he says are "after the elements of the world, and not after Christ" (Col. 2:8, mar.). The apostle's one remedy for dealing with these things is to tell the Colossians that they had *died with Christ* from the elements of the world," therefore they did not belong to this present world and the "childish lessons of outward things" were only meant as means to the end of leading the children of God to the knowledge of the things in the heavens (Col. 2:20, mar. and CH).

The cross and I myself.

> "I have been crucified with Christ; and it is no longer I that live, but Christ liveth in me: and that life which I now live in the flesh I live in faith, the faith which is in the Son of God, who loved me and gave Himself up for me" (Gal. 2:20).

In these words we have in concise and clear language the deepest secret of the cross, and the way of escape from the adversary and his power. Here again we find the sinner nailed to the cross with the Saviour, but this time with the innermost purpose fully shown. Deliverance by crucifixion with Christ from the claims of sin, from the desires of the flesh, from the elements of this present evil world—all these represent the negative side of escaping from the elements of the earth which have given the adversary his hold upon us. But now the *purpose* of the Lord in carrying the sinner to the cross is revealed: it is that Christ—the Risen Christ—may dwell in the one He has redeemed!

Now the meaning of the adversary's bitter fight against the cross, and his ceaseless efforts to hold the believer in the bonds of sin, the flesh or the world, is exposed. The prince of darkness cares little for the child of God, but he fears his Conqueror—the One who brought him to nought by His cross—and he dreads the hour when the truth dawns upon the redeemed one and the Living Christ is revealed in possession of the soul.

The Apostle Paul knew the secret and voiced his yearning over his converts in the words, "My little children, of whom I am again in travail until Christ be formed in you" (Gal. 4:19). But as much as Paul longed for this end, the adversary feared it. He knew that once the secret of the cross and the mystery of the indwelling Christ was apprehended, the believer would know the way to pass out of his power, and be kept by the power of God in the place where "the evil one toucheth . . . not."

"No longer I" is the very central point of deliverance. "I"—is the man himself retiring, so to speak, to the cross, to make room for the Risen Christ to dwell in him and live his life for him! "I"—is not only the sins, not only the works of the flesh, not only the present evil world, but *"myself."* "Let him take his cross and deny *himself,"* said the Lord Jesus to His disciples. "I myself" am on the cross, henceforth not to be taken into account, acknowledged, or given any place, or consideration at all. When the soul apprehends this meaning of Calvary, the Holy Spirit has reached the core of the life and the mainspring of action. All other things in some way may be said to lie in the circumference. The mainspring of "I" seems to lie even deeper than the heart, for we have found that the heart may be cleansed in its desires and motives, be truly indwelt by the Spirit, and yet "I" can still be plainly seen. The "works of the flesh" may be crucified in a great degree, and yet "I" hold the throne! In short, the believer may realize every aspect of the cross in deliverance from the bondage of sin, the works of the flesh, and the elements of the world without having apprehended the crucial meaning of the cross which the adversary most dreads—that apprehension of death with Christ, that Christ may be revealed within, and the life of Jesus manifested in the mortal flesh.

The truth is that there are deeps—abysmal deeps—in the death of Christ which no human being can fathom. "Baptized *into His death*" is no mere figure. *His death* took place on the cross. The Christ hanging there had in Him potentially all those who would afterwards believe into Him and experientially be baptized into His death. The Spirit of God must open to the believer these mysterious deeps of Calvary and submerge him ever deeper and deeper into Christ's death until, so to speak, he sinks out of sight into Him. Then the bonds of sin are broken, the desires of the flesh are crucified, and the elements of this present world fade further and further away. The child of God finds himself joined in strange oneness of identification with the crucified One on His cross. The sacrifice is bound with cords—mysterious cords—to the altar of the cross; it is drawn by the Spirit of God deeper and deeper into its depths, for identification is not a figment but a real spiritual fact, which is to be brought about in every one of the redeemed by the working of the Divine Spirit. A true union in death with Christ must of necessity precede a true union with His life. There are no theories in God's dealing with the world. Every word used in the Scriptures concerning Calvary and the believer's death with Christ, to sin, the flesh, the world, and the devil, stands for a spiritual verity which is to be actually brought about in the surrendered believer by the Holy Spirit. The work of Christ on the cross in all its aspects (excepting that of atonement) is to be wrought into the redeemed one for his actual deliverance and translation into the sphere of the Spirit in Christ Jesus. The righteousness imputed to the pardoned sinner is to be imparted by the inworking of the Divine Spirit.

It is when the believer is united to the crucified Lord on His cross, by ceaselessly retiring into Him by faith—made actual fact by the corresponding action of the Spirit—that the soulish life is hated and renounced and the believer learns to live moment by moment drawing upon the life of the Lord from heaven. What "I have been crucified with Christ" meant to Paul is shown in his succeeding words, "the life which *I now live in the flesh* [body] I live in the faith of the Son of God"—a life lived in continual dependence upon the Risen, Living Christ dwelling in him; drawing upon Him for all things, and not from the source of himself.

This is the deliverance of Calvary which the adversary most fears for the redeemed one to know, for it draws the believer right out of his reach by merging him out of sight into the crucified Lord, making way for the Christ Himself to possess the earthen vessel and manifest His life and power.

Then He draws His possessed one ever deeper and deeper into the fellowship of His sufferings and conformity to His death, while He quickens the whole being by His life and leads the soul into fuller knowledge of the ascension power of God.

CHAPTER SIX

*On the resurrection side of the cross. The call
to arms and the armor of light.*

THE clearest unveiling of life in the heavenly
sphere in Christ is given in the Epistle to the
Ephesians. Following aptly the letter to the
Galatians, which may be called the "crucifixion
Epistle," the letter to the Ephesians might in contrast be called the "Epistle of the heavenly life."
Paul, having heard of the faith in Christ of the
Ephesian Christians, prays that they may be given
a "spirit of wisdom and of insight," and have the
eyes of their hearts "illuminated" or "filled with
light," so that they might know their calling, and
"how surpassing is the power which He has shown
toward us who believe." This power is exemplified
"in the strength of that might wherewith He
wrought in Christ, when He raised Him from the
dead, and set Him on His own right hand in the
heavens, far above every Principality and Power,
and Might, and Domination," and "put all things
under His feet" (Eph. 1:17–22, CH).

Here the apostle clearly refers to the angelic

hierarchy which includes both the good and evil powers—for the angels of God all worship the Son of God (Heb. 1:6), and the hierarchy of evil powers are subject to Him. But most wonderful of all is the language used by the apostle concerning the redeemed sinner. The Father of Glory having manifested His surpassing might in raising from the dead the Prince of Life, "whom . . . they slew, hanging Him on a tree" (Acts 10:39), called those whom He thus redeemed to *"share the life of Christ"*; "in Christ Jesus, He raised us up with Him from the dead, and seated us with Him in the heavens" (Eph. 2:5–6, CH).

How truly we need the eyes of the "understanding being filled with light"—the light from heaven—to apprehend, and to appropriate, this marvelous revelation of the grace of God to fallen sinners!

We have already seen that the cross is the gate into this heavenly sphere, so that—if the Holy Spirit reveals to us that when we are submerged into the death of Christ, we are loosed from the claims of sin, the flesh, and the devil—He will as certainly impart to us the life of the Risen Lord; He will lift us in real experience into our place in Him, seated with Him in the heavens far above all principalities and powers. And the apostle writes to the Romans that if we have become partakers of a vital union— that is, *shared the reality of His death* (Rom. 6:5, Conybeare's note)—"so shall we also share His resurrection." Yes, if we consent to the sharing of His death, and yield to the Spirit for vital union with it, the sharing of His life assuredly follows: "like as Christ was raised from the dead through the glory of the Father" (Rom. 6:4), so He purposes that we likewise may know "newness of life." The original Greek means an *entirely new life essence,* an *essential inward* life, the resurrection life of Christ—the very same supernatural life which energized the Lord when He arose and emerged from the tomb!

It is important at this point to emphasize that at the beginning of the overcoming life—when we find deliverance from the bondage of sin—we may *apprehend* our union with the glorified Lord and our place of victory in Him, seated far above the powers of darkness; but *experientially* it is only as we are led on to know the meaning of the cross in its deeper aspects that we are brought fully into the life in Him, and really dwell in the heavenly sphere. This may be understood if we liken the cross to a knife which the Holy Spirit uses to sever the yielded believer from all things not of God. As the daily detaching and severing is done, the inner spirit is freed to rise more and more into closer essential union with Him who was raised from the dead by the glory of the Father.

The believer may be said to be an overcomer at every stage of his progress from death into life— but the ascension life of power over all the power of the enemy is known only when the Holy Spirit has triumphed at every point, and brought the soul into *entire conformity to the death of Christ* by the power of the resurrection which works within him. This conformity has to be maintained and deepened every moment as the condition of continued power. It is now that the believer understands the reality of the life in union with Christ, and how the Church, brought into her place in the heavenlies, is a testimony to the "principalities and powers in the heavens" of the manifold wisdom of God in His divine plan for the redemption of the fallen sons of men.

We now see the believer seated with Christ in the heavens, in the place of victory. But conflict is not ended; it is only changed in character and in place, and is quite distinct from the conflict described in Galatians 5. There it is a conflict between the indwelling Spirit and the flesh, when the believer had to put his will on God's side and affirm that they who were of Christ Jesus had crucified the flesh. But *now* the apostle writes to those who are united to Christ in the heavenly sphere, and he rings out

A CALL TO ARMS.

"Let your hearts be strengthened in the Lord, and in the conquering power of His might. Put on the whole armor of God, that you may be able to stand firm against the wiles of the devil. For the adversaries with whom we wrestle are not flesh and blood, but they are the Principalities, the Powers, and the Sovereigns of this present darkness, the spirits of evil in the heavens" (Eph. 6:10–12, CH).

Now it is a conflict with direct spiritual forces—a warfare with "spirits of evil" and aerial dignitaries possessed of supernatural power. The struggle appears to be mainly one of defense! A battle to "stand firm" against the onslaughts of the hosts of hell. The whole armor of God is needed for this battle with the aerial foes, for all the "wiles of the devil," the "fiery darts of the evil one," and the assaults of the spiritual hosts of wickedness will be directed against the believer to draw him out from his place in Christ back to the sphere of earth.

Why? There are many reasons which easily come to mind.

(1) Every believer who is brought into experiential deliverance through the cross and made to sit with Christ far above the hosts of darkness draws the whole Body of Christ heavenward. The converse is also terribly true, for every victory of Satan over the believer sends a shiver of defeat throughout the whole Church of God.

(2) The soul hidden with Christ in God has "authority over all the power of the enemy," for he shares in the victory of Christ. In Him he has power to tread on serpents and scorpions, and power to deliver and loose others from the bonds of the evil one.

(3) The soul united to the Risen Lord and dwelling in Him abides in Him by living in the searchlight of God—light *as God is in the light*—therefore he quickly discerns and exposes the "works of darkness," as Peter unveiled the devil at work in Ananias in Pentecostal days.

There are many other reasons, but these three suffice to show why all the "wiles" are planned to draw the believer out of his hiding place in the all-conquering Lord, back onto earthly ground; the "fiery darts" are flung in the hope of finding a place where they will fasten so as to give the evil one an entrance. Hence the necessity for putting on the whole armor of God, so that we may "stand firm" in our place of safety, and be able, in special onslaughts of the hosts of darkness—which the apostle calls the *evil day*—to "overthrow them all," and stand unshaken (Eph. 6:13, CH).

As to the forces engaged in the battle against even one soul entrenched in Christ, the whole army of hell—the prince of the aerial host, principalities, powers and spirits of evil, are of one mind in their fiendish aim of drawing the believer out of his hiding place in the Ascended Lord. It is vitally important that we do not underestimate the foe. From our place "in the Lord" we may calmly look at all that is against us, so that we may fully grasp the purpose of the adversary and see what he has to gain by victory. We also need to understand the tremendous consequences to the hosts of evil if we abide in victory, for all the power of the omnipotent God is behind us, and working through us, as we are united to Christ and encased within the panoply of God. "Authority . . . over all the power of the enemy" (Luke 10:19) is then actually true, for the Victor of Calvary identifies Himself with His possessed one, and through him will manifest the "conquering power of His might" over all the forces of hell.

It is necessary to understand also the *spiritual* character of the conflict, so that we cease to see "flesh and blood" as adversaries! Often the battle in the "evil day" of special attack is a wrestling of spirit with spirit, and at the time it may be impossible for the mind of the believer to distinguish between what is of his own spirit and what comes from the dark spirits of evil.

At other times the spiritual foe hides himself behind "flesh and blood"—as he did behind Peter, urging the Master to surrender to self-pity and shun the cross. But the soul who is walking in the light and encased in the armor of light will be given increasingly clear vision to detect the workings of the adversary behind all the covers he uses. With "senses exercised to discern" (Heb. 5:14), the believer will be able to stand firm against the foe's wiles, and by the shield of faith quench all his fiery darts from whatever quarter they come.

The Apostle Paul was a trained warrior in the conflict with the forces of hell, and from his letters we see how real the foe and the battle was to him, learning much about how to defeat the tactics of the evil one. "We are not ignorant of his devices" (2 Cor. 2:11), wrote the apostle, and the believer must not be ignorant if he is to abide in the place of victory—for in the heavenlies as well as on earth, the adversary works through ignorance. It is true spiritually as well as in the natural world: "In vain is the net spread in the sight of any bird" (Prov. 1:17). "Ye shall know the truth and the truth shall make you free" might also be written as *"and the truth shall keep you free"*; for to the soul walking with God, the same instant that the wiles of the devil are recognized, they are broken—provided the believer walks in integrity before God, desiring only His glory, and His will to be done.

This brings us to the "armor" which is a spiritual one, for protection from a spiritual foe.

THE ARMOR OF LIGHT

"Let us therefore cast off the works of darkness, and let us put on the armor of light . . . put ye on the Lord Jesus Christ" (Rom. 13:12, 14).

In the ringing call to arms with which the apostle concludes his letter to the Ephesians, he cries, "Put on the whole armor of God," and then repeats, "Take up with you to the battle the whole armor of God" (Eph. 6:11, 13, CH). All the language he uses speaks of decision and definite action! The *will* of the believer is always taken into account. The rebellious will which has fought so keenly against God, when surrendered and conquered by Him is not to be crushed and broken but re-energized by divine power and turned against the adversary. "Cast off the works of darkness," the apostle cries! Christ has conquered the prince of darkness and won liberty for the captives under his control. Take your liberty! "Cast off" the works of darkness, and behind your will you shall find the co-working of the Divine Spirit casting off your chains. "Put on the armor of light!" *Clothe yourselves* with the Lord Jesus Christ" (Rom. 13:14, CH). The "armor" is the Christ Himself, who emerged from the tomb Conqueror over death and hell. "Whosoever among you have been baptized *into Christ, have clothed yourself with Christ*" (Gal. 3:27, CH), writes the apostle to the Galatians. This links the cross and the armor together, for baptized into Christ means in spiritual significance being baptized *into His death.* The "clothing with Christ" cannot be meant to cover what is contrary to Christ, or it would be making the believer like the Pharisees who "outwardly appear beautiful, but inwardly are full of . . . all uncleanness" (Matt. 23:27–28). But the cross is again the key. The believer submerged into death, so that all which is contrary to Christ is *kept continually crucified,* is "clothed" as well as indwelt by the Risen Lord. Cast off darkness! Put on Christ as Light! Be planted into Christ on the cross, and you become clothed with Christ—the Armor of Light.

In his letter to the Ephesians, the old warrior Paul gives a fuller description of the armor, so that the believer may understand the various sections of it and take heed that no part is missing—otherwise the alert enemy will obtain a footing and win a victory. "Stand girt with the belt of *truth*, and wearing the breastplate of *righteousness*," and, cries the apostle, "shod as ready messengers of the glad tidings of *peace* . . . take up to cover you the shield of *faith* . . . take likewise the helmet of *salvation*, and the sword of the Spirit which is the *word of God*." How vividly these few details of the armor depict the conditions for victory!

The belt holds the armor in place, bound tightly to the figure, and the "girding" expresses readiness for work or conflict as the case may be. We have already seen how the truth makes one free because Christ is Truth, and the devil is a liar and a deceiver. The Lord can only be our armor while we walk in truth—*truth* first and foremost in everything: in the inward parts; in our attitude to God over sin; in our dealing with our fellow men. No prevarication can be tolerated, no willful giving of wrong impressions, no exaggeration of facts, no coloring of actions. Always, everywhere, in everything, at any cost or sacrifice, we need to be facing the truth as it concerns ourselves in the eyes of others and of God, looking to God with a keen desire for the light of His truth to be streaming upon us, within and without, day after day. In brief, truth is *light*, and untruth in any degree is darkness. The prince of darkness and of untruth is conquered by the soul abiding in the light of truth. Let us clearly understand, then, that victory depends on being girt with the belt of truth. Be aware that the devil's wiles will ceaselessly be planned to entangle us in some shade of untruth, whether in our attitude toward God or our intercourse with others.

The "breastplate of righteousness" is the next condition of victory. This may be briefly said to be a "conscience void of offense toward God and men" (Acts 24:16), for it is only when our heart does not condemn us that we have boldness toward God. The adversary knows this, and so is the "accuser of the brethren" seeking to bring the believer into condemnation before God. Decision is necessary here, as well as a knowledge of the power of the blood of the Lamb. Let the believer remember that the Lord Christ is a Faithful Witness and will faithfully tell His possessed ones the moment they are out of accord with His will. He is always *definite* in His dealings with His children, and the soul in fellowship with Him quickly knows when He speaks with the still, small voice of conscience—and must at once obey and claim the cleansing of the precious blood. The condemnation of the evil one is usually *vague*, but it too should be met by the believer claiming the constant cleansing of the blood. Hence doubtful things must be dealt with by a committal to the Lord—a trust that He will remove what comes from the accuser and will deepen and renew all that comes from Himself. The breastplate of righteousness will then be kept upon the heart to protect it from the foe.

The feet shod with the preparation of the gospel of peace, or "shod as ready messengers of the glad tidings," come next in the armor for conflict with the foe. The feet represent the walk on earth, demonstrating how much the "word of testimony" has to do with the life of victory. Following the belt of truth and the breastplate of righteousness, we see that a life of truth and fellowship with God is bound to *result in testimony*. "Shod as ready messengers" of the gospel! The one who dwells with Christ in the heavenlies walks on earth for the one and only purpose of being a ready messenger for Him, and for this part of the armor to be overlooked will mean defeat before the foe. The *whole* armor is necessary for victory, and all parts of it make up the whole. The soul who is an overcomer is therefore a messenger and cannot be an overcomer without obedience here.

Hastening hither and thither on the earth, bearing the message of the Lord, the armor-covered messenger now needs the "shield of faith" to "quench all the fiery darts of the evil one"; for he is moving in the realm of the adversary carrying messages to captives held by his power. We can almost see the dark prince or his minions following him, launching the "fiery darts," but he is covered by the shield of faith in the keeping of a faithful God. The darts tipped with fire from hell fall upon the believing one and they are quenched. But let a fiery dart fall and find the believer *questioning the keeping of God*—then how quickly the sting is felt! Now the "helmet of salvation" is necessary, for the "darts" are generally directed against the head, or the *thoughts.* An evil suggestion is shot in as an arrow to the mind, and the believer must quickly refuse it and claim "salvation," which is, in other words, the cleansing of the blood which was shed at Calvary. If the thought is not at once rejected and cleansed, it lies as a poisoned dart, unheeded at the time and later producing sad results.

How clearly the armor-covered believer now stands out to our gaze in the apostle's description.

See him girded with truth! The adversary fails to get him entangled here. His heart is in peace with no condemnation, for he knows nothing against himself; his conscience is void of offense toward God and men, with the blood of Jesus cleansing continually from all sin. See him with alacrity and joy giving the message of the glad tidings as he walks the earth, covered and protected by the shield of faith in the keeping power of God, who covers him with the whole armor of light. See the prince of darkness following him; note the hosts of wicked spirits watching him! See! Something happens in his path—he is injured, insulted or ignored. Now is the adversary's time! A "fiery dart" is winged—the thought flashes into the mind, "How unfair; how unjust. It is necessary that you speak—you must defend yourself for righteousness' sake!" Now is the time to "take the helmet of salvation." Quickly, *quickly* reject the thought and cry, "The blood of the Lamb cleanses."

But supposing the fiery dart is unheeded. At the moment it is not noticed, but it is there in the mind! It is a spark from hell. The enemy is content to let it lie. He has gained a spot from which he can act later on. Days pass, and the believer meets the one who injured him. A coldness comes over him, circumstances arise; before he is aware he finds himself in friction and resentment. The fiery dart has done its work, the breastplate of righteousness is gone, and defeat follows. Sorrow, confession, shame and restoration come next, but what a loss of time! It has been victory for the adversary and dishonor to the Lord! Yes, the helmet of salvation is needed for the protection of the *thoughts* and the retaining of the heart in peace.

Lastly in the hand, as the only offensive as well as defensive weapon, must be a sword! The sword of the Spirit which is the Word of God. The Christ-encased Christian must never parley with the foe, but only say "It is written" so and so, or "God hath said" this or that. The sword must be gripped, and the whole armor retained by "all prayer and supplication, praying at all seasons in the Spirit, and watching thereunto in all perseverance and supplication for all the saints." Moment by moment the armor of light encases the soul in answer to prayer! Never for one moment in any circumstances, or in any place, may the soul dare cease to pray and supplicate the protecting power of the Lord. "At all seasons in the Spirit . . . watching!" Never be off guard, for the enemy is never asleep, and yet you are not to guard yourself, but ceaselessly trust the guarding of the Lord. Your every breath must be a prayer—not only for your own victory, but for all the saints. Your victory is bound up with the victory of others; you cannot walk alone. Watch therefore, and be alert because the foe is watching you.

CHAPTER SEVEN

*The wiles of the adversary in the spiritual
sphere concerning revelations, the voice of the
Lord, guidance, and liberty.*

HAVING examined the various parts of the heavenly armor, let us see that we are now encased in it safely under the protection of the blood of the Lamb, as we take the sword of the Spirit, the Word of God, and unveil some of the wiles of the devil in some aspects of life in the spiritual sphere.

In a previous chapter we saw the way the Holy Spirit unveils the cross to the believer in liberating power, translating him out of the realm of darkness into the Kingdom of the Son of God. But there are many who enter the sphere of the Spirit without intelligent knowledge of how they were led in. Some will say that it was when they surrendered wholly to God that the Holy Spirit filled them and revealed the Risen Lord. Others that it was *suddenly*, and in response to a simple act of *faith*, that they received the Holy Spirit; and others again will tell of long seeking and deep anguish of heart, as the Divine Spirit searched and bent them to the dust. The truth is that absolute, unreserved surrender to God, and *faith* that God the Holy Spirit does enter and take possession, must bring response from Him, whether the believer's intellect understands or not the conditions of His indwelling. The Spirit of God also works in the soul according to the individual character and temperament. Some abandon themselves to Him more recklessly than others! Some see at a glance the crucial conditions for the effectual manifestation of His power and quickly enter a life of liberty, which others may reach by a slower and longer road.

One point is clear for all: those who enter the Spirit-sphere by intelligent apprehension of the meaning of the *cross* as the gate to life, and as the continuous cause of abundance of life, have a depth and permanency of experience which others fail to know. It is necessary to point this out in connection with the particular wiles of the devil to which the believer is exposed in the heavenlies, for those who know the cross know the only power which unveils the tactics of the evil one. Let us note first—

WILES CONCERNING "REVELATIONS."

"I know a man in Christ . . . caught up into Paradise" (2 Cor. 12:2–4).

"The manifestation of the Spirit is for profit" (1 Cor. 12:7, CH).

"I will love him, and will manifest Myself unto him" is a promise made by the Lord to His disciples on the eve of His cross and passion. He added "and My Father will love him, and We will come unto him and make Our abode with him" (John 14:21, 23). The disciples said, *How?* But after Pentecost they knew!

It is just the same with every believer who is led by the Spirit into union with the Living Christ. There is a moment when the promise is fulfilled, the Christ who rose from the dead reveals Himself to the obedient heart, and the believer knows the Risen Lord. To some He appears in light above the brightness of the sun, as to Paul in a wondrous heavenly vision; others are but conscious of His presence in peace and unspeakable joy. Some are "caught up into Paradise." Others fall at His feet as dead, or can only cry like Isaiah "Woe is me," or like Job "Mine eye seeth Thee, wherefore I abhor myself." In any case, the Glorified Christ now becomes a living, bright reality to the soul. What are the wiles of the adversary now but an attempt to impersonate the Lord! The believer must know that the evil one can fashion himself as an angel of light and work with all "power and signs and lying wonders" (2 Thess. 2:9) to lead astray if he possibly can the very elect. Alas, some have found to their bitter cost that he is able to give "manifestations" and "visions" of heavenly things.

The believer is in a new world, ignorant of the subtlety of the foe. The adversary will now watch his opportunity to counterfeit the working of the Spirit, and he waits but for an *element of self* to manifest itself in the believer in order to gain his end. If he seeks "visions and revelations" for his *own* enjoyment the adversary will give them, for the Holy Spirit cannot respond to any desire but for the glory of the Lord. It is here that the knowledge of the cross is the safeguard, for then the believer knows that "crucified with Christ" is the only hope for keeping him from the snares of the foe.

The one who would walk in victory must also take heed not to glory in, or boast of, his experiences. Often he may not even tell them without opening the door to the evil one. In the second letter of the Apostle Paul to the Corinthians we find that he felt it necessary to draw a veil over this aspect of his inner life. "I forbear to speak," he said, "that I may not cause any man to think of me more highly than when he sees my deeds, or hears my teaching" (2 Cor. 12:6, CH). He knew how men were disposed to "glory in men" and account them wonderful, as the Lycaonians did Barnabas and himself when they saw the miracle of healing done in the crippled man in answer to their simple words. "We are men of like nature with you," the apostles cried as with horror they sought to prevent them giving them the worship due to God alone (Acts 14:8–15, mar.).

In this letter we also see the means used by the Lord to counterbalance the danger to the earthen vessel of "abundance of revelations," in that Paul is given a "stake in the flesh," a "messenger of Satan" to buffet him, so that he might not be exalted excessively. The Lord's plan fulfilled its purpose, for the apostle is kept broken and humbled, saying, "I rather glory in my weaknesses . . . in injuries, in necessities, in persecutions, in distresses for Christ's sake: for when I am weak, then am I strong" (2 Cor. 12:9–10).

We need to walk carefully with God at this stage of the spiritual life and hide very deeply in the cross, not coveting wonderful experiences but rather an ever-deepening conformity to the death of Jesus—that the life of Jesus may be manifested to all around (2 Cor. 4:10–11). Let us know too that our faith is more precious to God than gold, being content to walk by faith not sight. We need to remember also that "visions and revelations" are not given to the soul for its own comfort or enjoyment. They serve some definite purpose in the counsels of God, or appear in a special and critical time of need, as with the Apostle Paul when he was stoned in Lystra (2 Cor. 12 agrees in date with this time), called to Macedonia, or needed clear guidance to remain in Athens. But normally, as the believer matures, the "eyes of his heart"—the *spiritual power of sight* possessed by the inner man of the new creation—must be more and more filled with light. Thus the spiritual vision becomes acute and able to see the things of the spiritual world, not so much by "revelations" as by the simple power of *seeing,* a faculty of the new man which is called by Paul "discernment." "Full-grown men" in the spiritual life, "by reason of use have their senses exercised to discern good and evil" (Heb. 5:14). So the believer "walks in the light, as [God] is in the light," and the light makes manifest, or reveals all things around him. At all stages of experience let the one who would walk in safety in the Spirit-sphere test all visions and revelations by direct appeal to the Spirit, to apply the power of the death of Christ, which disperses all that may come from the adversary fashioned as an angel of light. Then quickly any counterfeit will fade away, and the believer will press on victoriously over all wiles of the devil.

WILES CONCERNING THE VOICE OF GOD.

"The sheep follow Him: for they know His voice ... they know not the voice of strangers" (John 10:4–5).

These words clearly show that the Lord does speak to His children, and that He makes them able to distinguish His voice from the voice of strangers. They know His as a babe knows its mother's voice, but like the babe, they may not be able to say how or why. When the believer is brought by the Spirit into the Spirit-sphere, and Christ is manifested to him, one of the first results is the voice of the Lord in the heart, speaking in a way the soul has never realized before. How unspeakably sweet and precious is this voice; none can understand save those who know it and have realized how even one word pierces deep into the very joints and marrow of the life—satisfying, calming, strengthening and quickening by its power. "It is the voice of my Beloved . . . and my heart was moved within me" (Song 5:2, 4, mar.), cries the soul who from this time feels it is the one thing in life for him to obey and heed the voice of the Lord—for the inner ear of the heart to be kept open to catch the faintest whisper of His will.

In the early days the adversary knows that the believer has but little knowledge of his foe. Satan soon plans wiles to counterfeit the voice of the Lord, so as to confuse or to mislead. He purposes either to *destroy faith in the guidance of the Spirit* or else to lead the believer into obedience to the voice of the devil—to strong delusion into believing a lie, thinking it to be the truth of God.

The adversary works through our ignorance, and the believer must know how to distinguish the voice of the Lord from the voice of the foe. This is done: (1) by its sound, (2) by its effect, (3) by its object. Elijah describes the voice of the Lord as "a

sound of gentle stillness" (1 Kings 19:12, mar.),
whereas the adversary's voice is always harsh. So
gently does the Lord speak that the heart must be
in great stillness to hear His voice. It seems to come
from what we may describe as the central depth of
the spirit . . . where the Lord is enthroned. But the
voice of the adversary is loud, and appears generally to ring more in the outward ear with a metallic
sound, endeavoring to force the soul to hasty actions. We need then to remember the character of
the Holy Spirit who is depicted as a dove, and
recollect that He never forces or drives but leads
the yielded heart gently into all the will of God; the
evil one hurries and pushes until we are compelled
to obey the urgent voice, almost for the sake of
peace! The voice of the Lord, too, brings a deep
calm over the spirit and a quiet assurance of the
will of God, whereas the voice of the devil often
causes restlessness, agitation and uncertainty.
Again the voice of the Lord is invariably in accord
with the teaching of the Word of God and generally speaks in the words of Scripture. The adversary also can quote Scripture, as he did to the Lord
Himself in the wilderness, but he usually quotes
texts with the portions omitted which safeguard or
interpret the whole, or else he uses isolated words
wrenched from the context which explains them!

The lying voice of the evil one also aims at bring-
ing the soul into bondage to minute trifles, instead
of into the glorious liberty of the children of God. It
is not that the Lord overlooks the importance of
careful walking in His will, but He desires to obtain the intelligent cooperation of His redeemed
ones, rather than their blind obedience as if they

were but machines. He watches them with eyes of love and only speaks to direct their steps when He sees them likely to miss the path. Again we must notice that the wiles of the adversary are the most subtle, and likely to succeed, in the early days of the life in the Spirit-sphere. As the believer matures in the knowledge of God, the Lord speaks more rarely—as the *"mind of Christ"* becomes the very mind of the one in fellowship with God.

It is well that the believer should understand this, lest he give advantage to the enemy by falling into discouragement or depression when the transition from childhood to manhood takes place. In the early days the voice of the Lord was so sweet that the believer was well content to obey it as a little child; but the life of Christ in him has been growing more rapidly than he was aware, and now the voice that guided him has not spoken for a long time. "My Father, have I fallen away from Thee, that Thou dost not speak?" he cries!

The answer comes, "What is in thy *mind*, My child, toward this or that?"

"This looks the right course to take," the child-like heart replies.

And the word comes back, "Ye *have the mind of Christ*—do what is in thy mind!" The believer understands that from then on shall be fulfilled in him that which is written in the Scripture of truth, "The meek He will guide in judgment [and] teach His way." This brings us to consider—

THE WILES CONCERNING GUIDANCE.

"As many as are led by the Spirit of God, these are sons of God. For ye received not the spirit of bondage . . . but . . . the spirit of adoption, whereby we cry, Abba, Father" (Rom. 8:14–15).

There is scarcely any subject connected with the spiritual life more difficult to explain and more misunderstood than the subject of guidance! The words "I was led to do this or that" are so often used when there is no evidence of any leading at all. For instance, several letters will say that each of the writers felt "led" to ask the same person to speak simultaneously at meetings in different places, so that obviously all were not under the true leading of the Spirit!

And yet it cannot be that the Father in heaven has made it difficult for His children to know His will. The truth is that guidance is simple to the childlike heart but difficult to the wise and prudent, who lean to their own understanding and make perplexities by their own reasonings and the multiplicity of their thoughts.

Let us note some of the wiles of the adversary, and then look at some of the conditions for walking in the will of God. One tactic of the evil one is to make souls confused and distracted over what is the will of God, for he knows that a tranquil heart is necessary for the leading of the Spirit; others he deludes into throwing aside all use of their judgment and knowledge to act upon some isolated text or some thought that came to them in prayer! Others again who are truly shown by the Spirit the will of God for their own path are beguiled into an attitude of judgment upon the walk of others and think themselves not far short of infallibility, though they would not use the word! Then there is the fine line between faith and presumption which the devil always tries to blur; we must learn where the passivity, necessary for God's mightiest working through us, becomes fatalism—and where creaturely activity hinders the Spirit working effectually through us.

Just as with the wiles concerning revelations and the inner voice, the matter of guidance is more open to the workings of the adversary in the early stages of the life in the heavenlies. The dread of "going back into the flesh" often drives the believer to extremes; for a time he throws aside all *mental* food, forgetting that the Lord redeemed the whole man—spirit, soul and body—and that he consists of something more than spirit! All culture of the intellect is neglected and the life is thrown into one groove, until the body rebels and nature asserts her claims.

But the soul who will rely on the Lord as a little child will be brought safely through the dangers of its early days. Our text gives in a few words the principal mark of the true guidance of the Lord. "*Led* by the Spirit" means that He *leads,* and does not drive or force; therefore the soul must take heed not to force itself into any course of action which is repugnant to it—that is, *presupposing that the will is surrendered to God as ready to take any course unmistakably shown to be His will.* This is an important point, one to which souls who have really been taken into one life with Christ in the heavenlies should take special heed. Some have failed to recognize the Spirit restraining them from taking a certain path, thinking it was the devil hindering their way! The text again meets this aspect, for it is written "As many as are led . . . they are *sons* of God"! They know God as a Father as the spirit of bondage has passed away. They now cry

"Father," and walk with God as a Father because they partake of the nature of His Son. "God sent forth the Spirit of His Son into our hearts, crying, Abba, Father," so that you are "no longer a bondservant, but a son." Remember, as a *son* the Spirit will lead you and work in you to want to do His will. You must never force yourself into any path against inward restraint; but if you fear the adversary, you may claim the power of Calvary to clear the path, and trust the Spirit to draw you into it with all your heart, soul and strength—causing you to bound toward the will of God.

Let us also understand that as the life of Christ matures in the believer, the Spirit leads more from *within* by the working of a *life;* this new life manifests itself as simply and naturally as the life of nature. The actions of the body moved by the physical life are mainly unconscious and, to a certain extent, instinctive! So when the believer becomes a "full-grown man," with heart and will fully possessed by God as his whole being is under the complete control of the Spirit, the new life will increasingly work in him with less and less *perceived action* to his consciousness. As many as are led by the Spirit, in this way, are indeed sons of God, with spirit, soul and body working out His will with ease and spontaneity. (1) They are "guided by the skillfulness of His hands" (Ps. 78:72) upon them, moving them hour by hour into the path prepared for them. (2) They are guided by their faithfulness to God—"The integrity of the upright shall guide them" (Prov. 11:3)—for they know what to do by the very instincts of right and wrong which God has planted within them. (3) The "meek will He guide in judgment" (Ps. 25:9, KJV), for He uses their renewed minds (Rom. 12:2), giving them the very mind of Christ which led Him to empty Himself and be obedient unto death—the death of the cross. The believer who knows this principle of sacrifice and self-effacement as the characteristic of the life of Christ manifested in him *needs no inner voice nor special guidance to tell him what course he is to take* while walking in this present evil world!

There are times however, in all stages of experience for the Spirit-possessed believer, when special guidance is needed, as clear knowledge of the will of God must be known. Only a few hints on the way of obtaining this are possible here.

(1) *There must be no hidden sin, or disobedience to the known will of God,* if true guidance is to be obtained from the Lord in any emergency. Perhaps here the evil one will torture honest hearts, but the question can be quickly and easily settled if there is any doubt. Let the seeker go before the Lord and, waiting before Him, ask Him as the Faithful Witness to bring to mind anything in heart or life contrary to His will, or any unwitting step taken which has grieved Him. If the soul is honest before God, and ready to put away at once anything which is revealed, the faithful Lord is certain to reveal it. If nothing is shown after this honest seeking of the face of God, let the believer count upon the present cleansing of the precious blood of Jesus and rejoice in access to the throne of grace.

(2) *There must be no bias of the will* toward one course or the other in the matter on which guidance is sought. The will should be like the compass needle, turning toward the Lord as the needle turns

to the north no matter which way the compass is held. The very least "desire" toward one way or another in a debatable course prevents obtaining the mind of the Lord. The believer seeking guidance should therefore wait before the Lord for His light to reveal the attitude of the will before Him; an act of surrender may be necessary on the point where any bias is discovered. There is a stage of maturity in the Spirit-filled life in which the will is so truly one with God that it has no desire outside of His will. This means that deep Gethsemane experiences, and fellowship with Christ in His sufferings, have been passed through until the soul is one with Christ in God. Let the believer take special heed to this point of a surrendered will, for many have often sought their own will, thinking it to be the will of God.

(3) *There must be no preconceived plan in the mind* if true light from God is to be obtained. How many ask to be "led" after they have made their plans, instead of going to Him with open minds. But here again there is a danger of the adversary creating bondage. A "plan" may be taken to the Lord if suggested by others, but the seeker must himself be careful to keep an open mind and an obedient heart to carry out the light the Lord sheds upon the plan submitted to Him. We may note again here that, as the life matures and the will of God becomes deeply the will of the believer, he finds that he may lay before the Lord personal tastes and preferences, which are wholly separate from the attitude of the will and are subservient to the choice of the Lord.

(4) *There must be no preconception of the way in which the Lord will give the guidance sought.* Many

expect the Lord to answer in their particular way—
by a voice, or revelation, or text, or through a particular circumstance or person; in this way they are
not able to discern His guidance if it comes in any
other way. If He does not work according to their
ideas, they think He does not work at all! They
have sought guidance, they say none has been
given, and so they cast away their confidence,
sometimes drifting into a life of chaos and perplex-
ity with no assurance of the presence of God. But
the soul who truly desires His will must leave the
Lord complete freedom to work in any way that He
shall choose.

(5) *There must be absolute trust in the faithfulness of
God, that He does hear and does respond to the soul that
seeks His will.* The fulfillment of all the previously
named conditions of guidance are fruitless if the
seeker fails here, for "he that cometh to God must
believe that He is, and that He is a rewarder of
them that seek after Him." Granted that there is no
hidden sin, no known disobedience, no bias of desire toward one course or another, no preconceived
plan, no previous idea of the way that God will
guide, then let the one who seeks to have the mind
of God revealed to him:

1. Enter the Holy Presence boldly, pleading the
blood of Jesus and believing that it cleanses him
now—Hebrews 10:19.

2. Look up into the face of God as a Father in
Christ Jesus, who bends His ear to listen to the
words of His child.

3. Spread the need before Him in simplicity, as
if talking to a father on earth and pouring out his
heart concerning the various difficulties and points

of need.

4. Then definitely commit the whole matter into His hand, to work out for the best from the standpoint of His clearer vision and knowledge of all things concerned.

5. Yield the whole being to Him for His use in answering the prayer, for His highest purposes to be fulfilled in the seeker and the circumstances.

6. Then calmly, restfully trust all with God and leave Him to guide into His will in His own way. Trust Him to work in man's will to will His will. Trust Him to work out through the life in practical obedience. Trust Him to sway the affections into the right direction. Trust Him to guide the judgment into clear decision. Trust Him to restrain quickly if one is turning toward the wrong.

7. Now let the trusting one calmly, quietly believe that God is faithful, that God is guiding. Then take the next step that lies in the path of duty— "do the next thing"! Should no step be clear, let him wait in peace, quietly trusting that God is faithful and will not fail His child. Should the path continue in darkness, let him not cast away the confidence which will have sure reward. "Let him trust in the name [or character] of the Lord, and stay upon his God."

There are also certain principles governing the leading of the Lord which the matured believer learns to know, those which materially assist in obtaining guidance in any special time of need.

(1) The Holy Spirit will not lead into any step directly contrary to the written Word and to the character of God as revealed therein. Therefore, when any action is proposed which would cause

the enemies of the Lord to blaspheme, or be in any way dishonoring to Him, there is no need to seek "guidance" in the matter—the course should be instantly rejected.

(2) The Holy Spirit will always confirm any step He has led us into, by His presence and His accompanying blessing in the matter. For instance, He led Peter to go to the house of Cornelius contrary to all that the other apostles would have advised; but the Spirit bore witness that He had really led Peter there by pouring out His blessing in such measure that his brethren had to acknowledge that it was of God. We must learn therefore, in walking with God, to *prove* His will step by step and watch for His witness that we are in the right path. When He leads He goes before and makes the rough places plain and the crooked things straight. We may well doubt any "leading" into a course of action where we do not find the seal of God's presence and blessing.

(3) The Holy Spirit Himself must bear witness to others of our being led of Him. It does not seem in accord with the pattern-life of Jesus that we should be constantly *asserting* the leading of God; even the Lord Jesus did not say "I was led" to this or that, but to the brothers who pressed Him to go to the feast He simply said, "My time has not yet come"! It ill becomes any child of God to take any infallible position of guidance and assert too emphatically absolute certainty to others. To the world we are but human fallible beings; it therefore seems best to let God set His seal in His own way on those He possesses and truly leads.

(4) The Holy Spirit Himself is responsible to bring about the fulfillment of His plans. It is for

Him to lead and the soul to follow! Therefore there should be no "push," or creaturely activity, to bring about *what has been shown us as the mind of the Lord.* God has a time as well as a plan. Yet how many who have been shown by the Lord His will for them think that they must at once act to bring about His plan! Let the Spirit prove His revealed will by making iron gates open of their own accord for the soul who is ready to follow. He is a God who works for those who wait for Him. Let us wait upon Him, and follow as He goes first to open the way which He has revealed as His will. The knowledge of these things will defeat the wiles of the adversary, for the evil one knows that the armor of light can encase the soul only while he walks in the path marked out for him by the Lord. Hence Satan's wiles are planned to imitate the voice of the Lord so as to confuse, mislead, or to ensnare in guidance, in this way drawing the believer out of the keeping power of God, leading him into any suitable snare. Let the one who would live an overcoming life keep carefully to the written Word of God and depend as a child upon the Lord. Then He who was given to guide into all truth will teach the trusting heart, keeping him guarded by the power of God. This brings us lastly to—

WILES CONCERNING LIBERTY.

"Ye have been called unto liberty; only use not liberty for an occasion to the flesh, but by love serve one another" (Galatians 5:13, KJV).

The believer who has emerged into the life in the Spirit finds himself free in a way he has never known before. The spirit of bondage has passed away and he feels like the bird let go "into the open

field." It is just now that the evil one is ready with
new wiles to ensnare him, suggesting: (1) you have
liberty now to do anything, for you are free; or (2)
you are under no man's control now, especially
those who are "in the flesh"! And the adversary
does his best to counterfeit true freedom in Christ
by inciting rebellion to those in authority and stir-
ring up fleshy zeal under the name of the liberty of
the Spirit. But the Word of God is the safeguard
which unveils the tactics of the adversary, for it
shows that the liberty wherewith Christ makes us
free is really freedom from slavery to sin and the
evil one. The freed soul passes under *law to Christ*,
under the perfect law of liberty, which is liberty to
do right instead of *seeing* what is right and *doing*
what is wrong. Liberty to obey God instead of dis-
obeying Him. Heavenly liberty, which the angels
have in fulfilling His commands with ease and
joy—the will of God done on earth in us as it is
done in heaven! It is freedom to do what we like in
truth, when *we like only to please God!* "Ye have been
called unto liberty," writes the apostle to the
Galatians, but "use not liberty for an occasion to
the flesh, but by love serve." He that is "called free,
is Christ's bondservant" (1 Cor. 7:22). *Free to serve* is
the joy of the angels—this is liberty.

The believer is now free to do many things that
once he feared to do, so this is the time for the
adversary to endeavour to obtain an occasion for
the flesh. The law of Christ comes in here to show
that there is a limitation placed on liberty and that
limit is defined by the conscience of the weak
brother. The freed one is not only to be subject to
others in authority for the Lord's sake, but is to

take heed lest his liberty of action becomes "a stumblingblock to the weak" (1 Cor. 8:9). "All things are lawful" to the child of God, but "not all things edify" (1 Cor. 10:23). You must "abstain from every appearance of evil" (1 Thess. 5:22, mar.) and "let not your good be evil spoken of" (Rom. 14:16), but "take thought for things honorable in the sight of all men" (Rom. 12:17). The spirit of the cross calls us to sacrifice, requiring that the believer must often sacrifice his *liberty*, as well as his life, to gain men for Christ. This is very different from worldly expediency, for it is sacrifice for *others*, which must be the motive of every life lived in fellowship with Christ. "How things look to others" when our self-credit is at stake is altered when it is for the honor and character of Him whose name is upon us in the eyes of the world.

The Apostle Paul set an example for the believer, writing, "I have not used my right, but forego every claim, lest I should by any means hinder the course of Christ's glad tidings" (1 Cor. 9:12, CH and note). The meaning of the word "claim" is "to hold out against"—he would not "hold out" for his rights, but forego everything for himself rather than hinder the gospel. How careful, too, he was in the handling of money which was placed in his care. He did not trade upon his position as an apostle, nor ask unlimited confidence from others because of his wonderful spiritual experience. Rather he writes frankly to the Corinthians that he had taken all precautions that "no man should blame us" in the matter of administering the gift of money sent by his hand to the needy saints.

Let the believer who would walk in victory take

heed and forego all lawful rights which are not
expedient for the sake of the gospel. Let what is
good never have the appearance of evil, or be vul-
nerable to be evil spoken of, but in all things take
thought as to what practical action is honorable
and commendable to all men, "for so is the will of
God, that by well-doing ye should put to silence
the ignorance of men [who would not understand
your 'liberty']: as free, and not having your freedom for a cloke. . ." (1 Pet. 2:15–16, mar.). Even
thus did the Lord Christ sacrifice His liberty for the
sake of others, saying, "The sons are free, but lest
we cause them to stumble, go . . ." (Matt. 17:26–27).
Also in the Jordan He submitted Himself to bap-
tism by John with the words, "Thus it becometh us
to fulfill all righteousness" (Matt. 3:15).

CHAPTER EIGHT

The overcomer on the throne of victory; Satan
under the feet of the believer.

WE have now traced the story of the translation of a soul out of the "power of darkness" into the Kingdom of the Son, through the gate of death into resurrection life in union with the Risen Lord. We heard the call to arms, and the putting on of the heavenly armor to meet the new tactics of the foe, when the believer emerges into the spiritual sphere; and we have considered some of the wiles of the devil suited to the Spirit-filled believer. In closing we must see the way of victory and the place of authority over all the power of the enemy, which makes the redeemed one terrible as an army with banners to the foe.

When the believer emerges into the Spirit-sphere on the resurrection side of the cross, he enters into conflict with the aerial hosts of darkness who swarm in the region immediately surrounding our planet. Here he needs the whole armor of God to encase and protect him. Also we are taught that he has a place above them where he sits with Christ in

His place of victory "far above all principality, and power, and might, and dominion, and every name that is named" (Eph. 1:21–22, KJV), where Satan and all his hosts are under his feet. United to the Conqueror of Calvary, he sits and reigns with Christ in spirit, as he will do visibly to the world in the day when Christ shall appear in glory. Christ's victorious ones shall reign with Him a thousand years.

The call from heaven by the victorious Lord to His redeemed ones is a call to overcome as He overcame. And it is a promise that they who thus overcome shall sit with Him in His throne, even as He sat down a Victor over sin and death and hell, on His Father's throne. The believer is to enter into the victory of the Victor of Calvary, where through death He destroyed him who had the power of death, that is the devil. On Calvary's cross the God-man, beset with the powers and principalities of darkness, stripped them off and triumphed over them in His death (Col. 2:15); He ascended through their realm and passed to the throne, there to sit at the right hand of God waiting until His enemies become His footstool. Stage after stage of the believer's progress from the cross to the throne is shown in the messages to the seven churches, with the special rewards obtained at every stage. After emerging through the gate of the cross comes: (1) life in union with the Risen Lord; (2) victory over death in the path of tribulation; (3) a new nature and new character symbolized by the hidden manna and white stone; (4) authority over the nations, and the reigning life; (5) the clothing with Christ as in white garments; (6) the life within the veil; (7) and then the throne-life victory with Christ in God (Rev. 2:7, 11, 17, 26; 3:5, 12, 21).

What now are the practical conditions for realizing and abiding in the place of victory "far above" all the principalities and powers? All conditions for knowing and retaining the place of power are wrapped up in the one word—Calvary!

The cross on Calvary's hill was, for the God-man who triumphed there, the Victor's throne over all the principalities and powers of hell. And in heaven again the slain Lamb is seen to be in the midst of the throne. The altar and the throne are one. Neither can be divided from the other. The believer can only know the throne of victory by complete submergence into the death of Christ on the cross.

Calvary has *freed all things* from the prince of this world—potentially. The triumphant Lord on the throne now calls His Church to enter into His death, His life, and His throne-life of victory. Let the believer who has been translated out of the power of darkness into the Kingdom of the Son now yield to the Holy Spirit to be drawn into the death of Christ until, in deepening conformity to His death, he becomes assimilated to Him in vital union, even to oneness with His melted and broken heart. Let the yielding one cry out to the Spirit day by day to fulfill in him the utmost victory of Calvary over sin, self, death, and hell—and he will then find the reigning life of Jesus manifested in him in ever-increasing power over all things around him. While in union with the reigning Lord, he will find His ascension power drawing him ever more and more with Christ into God.

For *abiding* in the place of victory, Calvary again

is the key. All the powers of hell will be directed toward drawing the soul out of its hiding place in Christ on the cross and the throne—hence the endeavors of the adversary to arouse the workings of the life of nature in the believer, or others around him. The death in Christ separates one from the natural sphere of earth, and the life-union with Christ draws the soul into the supernatural sphere of the Spirit. Victory over known sin is now a settled matter in the walk of the believer who has followed his Lord thus far; it is now the realm of the life of nature which offers the opportunity to the adversary for his devices. The life which flows in us from the first Adam is a poisoned life and is the ground for the devil's workings.

The life of the Second Adam alone cannot offer material for the devices of the evil one. The cross of Calvary is the one safeguard and "shutter," so to speak, between the believer united to Christ and the touch of the life of earth. The severing power of the death of Christ is a continuous necessity if the soul is to abide with Christ in God. "Always bearing about the dying of Jesus"—yes, the cross severs the believer every moment from all that Christ died to free him from. It severs from sin and the desire for sin; it severs from the world and from the devil; and it severs from the life of the first Adam, which is the material for the devil to attack and work upon.

The abiding in the severing death of the cross *every moment* is therefore the supreme necessity for the soul who desires victory. And, be it remembered, the severing of the cross is not an actual experience unless the will of the believer desires and consents to separation in fact and practice. The cross only severs that from which we consent to part. Here lies the fight of the adversary, who seeks to throw upon the redeemed one desires for various things in the life of nature, in order to cause him to descend from the plane of the Spirit and of victory. *But Calvary is victory!* Hidden from the foe in the death of Him who conquered the devil by death, the believer is safe; as he abides he is led on day by day into fellowship with the Lamb slain, who is in the midst of the throne of God. Here Satan is under the feet of the Victorious Lord, who now sends forth His own to loose other captives from their bonds. Now encased in Christ, and wielding His authority, the reigning soul can command all the hosts of hell—as it is written, "The spirits are subject unto you." "Behold I have given you authority to *tread* . . . ," authority *"over"* all the power [or authority] of the enemy, and nothing shall in any wise hurt you" (Luke 10:19). Here "He that was begotten of God keepeth him, and the evil one toucheth him not" (1 John 5:18). May God lead every one of His children into the fullest victory of the cross, and thence to the throne, to overcome as the Lord Christ overcame and thus reign in life with Him here and beyond the veil, unto the ages of ages.

Particulars of the magazine *The Overcomer* may
be obtained from:

The Overcomer Literature Trust
9–11 Clothier Road
Brislington, Bristol BS4 5RL
England